A MONTH

A
MONTH
OF
SUNDAYS

Thirty-one prayers for
each of five
movements in
Christian worship

Jamie
Wallace

HODDER AND STOUGHTON
LONDON SYDNEY AUCKLAND TORONTO

ACKNOWLEDGMENTS

Thanks are due

to the Baptist Union's Department of Ministry whose sabbatical leave scheme, together with Dr Williams's Trust, helped to provide the leisure for compiling *A Month of Sundays* and its companion volume *There's a Time and a Place*.

to the British and Foreign Bible Society for permission to quote scripture texts from *Good News Bible* published by the Bible Societies/Collins, © American Bible Society 1976.

British Library Cataloguing in Publication Data

Wallace, Jamie
   A month of sundays – (Hodder Christian paperback)
   1. Prayer
   I. Title
   248.3'2   BV210.2

   ISBN 0-340-34819-4

CONTENTS

INDEXES

*For Joan and Jim Chadwin who put me up on the
way to Glasgow;
for Sally and Maurice Lillie who put me up
on the way back;
and for Una and Alan Stoddart who put up with
me while I was there.*

J.W.

FOREWORD

by the Ven. Bazil Marsh,
Archdeacon of Northampton

Some centuries ago, St Francisco de Usuna urged: Let us fan the fires of our devotion with the fresh breeze of delightful words. My judgment is that the great and widespread renewal of Christians which we see today owes much to those like Michael Quoist, Barclay, Micklem and Frank Colquhoun, who have found us fresh, true and delightful words to say when we speak to God in love. Those who read and use *A Month of Sundays* will find in Jamie Wallace's prayers a further and valuable resource of this kind.

Those considering acquiring a book of this sort will want to find that its prayers are theologically sound. They will hope for prayers which have grown out of a rich experience of Biblical facts, language and imagery, which will point them again and again to the God who is, and who is known in Christ Jesus. They will be looking for the language of true love, not formal or stilted, but contemporary, simple and evocative. They will want prayers which will relate as much to them as they actually are as they relate truly to God as he is. If they do acquire and use *A Month of Sundays*, they will not be disappointed.

These prayers have grown out of Jamie Wallace's ministry of many years to the praying congregation of a Northampton Baptist church, but that fact seems to me to be relevant only in so far as it goes to explain why they have such an authentic ring to them.

While they might be described as tailor-made for Free Church worship, I can see them being most useful in

churches accustomed to liturgical worship, where the
newer liturgies provide room for additional matter, and
in any church in non-liturgical services, small group
worship and in private devotion.

Composing prayers needs something of the art of the
poet, whose words we appreciate because we feel they
say what we mean and understand, but which in fact
open our hearts and gently lead us to truths which cannot
be expressed in words. Prayers in words are good and
useful if they provide us with that sort of stepping stone
to the prayer without words in which the Spirit conveys
the deep yearnings of our hearts to God. I have used
some of the prayers in this book. They have done it for
me. I am confident they can do it for many others.

BAZIL MARSH

INTRODUCTION

About the Prayers

This collection of prayers is the by-product of research into Free Church worship. My own practice as a minister in pastoral charge could be neither spared from scrutiny, nor ignored as evidence. So I studied *inter alia* the shape and content of the Sunday services I had prepared for my middle-sized, downtown, South Midland Baptist church in the ten years from 1971 to 1980.

Using the Prayers

The prayers selected are ones to which I have returned more than once: sometimes to use them again as they stood, sometimes to adapt them for a different occasion (*Beginning* 25 and 25b supply an example), sometimes taking from them as a starting point no more than an evocative phrase or an undeveloped thought.

Without the work of the Holy Spirit, Christian worship cannot happen, and he brings order, not chaos. Therefore in that tradition of worship which eschews control by rubric, no less than in that which does not, order is apparent. I found that each prayer I had written for public worship seemed to belong in one or another of five essential movements:

1 *Beginning*. The congregation *locates* itself, taking bearings on its own life, on God (relating itself to him gratefully – because he is good – and penitently, because we are not), and on its faith which is later

recapitulated more fully in sermon or sacrament or both.

2 *Family awareness*. Room is made in worship for the congregation to remind itself that it is a community with no upper or lower age limit.

3 *Self-offering*. The third movement is aptly symbolised in the giving of money and of the Communion bread and wine.

4 *Intercession*. In this movement the congregation exercises its priestly function, or, in a treasured phase, 'the priesthood of all believers'.

5 *Commitment and petition*. For the congregation and for its individual members, worship reaches an inner climax: in a renewed sense of the believer's privileged standing in the sight of God, as redeemed by grace, through faith. At this point the renewal of our self-consecration to God, and the urgent presentation to him of our deepest need, are inseparable.

This is not necessarily the time sequence of the movements, but such is their logical and devotional sequence. It has suggested the arrangement of the prayers in this book.

It is as a resource able to be drawn upon in a free and varied way, that I hope *A Month of Sundays* may prove useful to others.

JAMIE WALLACE

College Street Baptist Church, Northampton

ABOUT THE AUTHOR

Jamie Wallace comes of an extended family whose latest three generations have included Roman Catholics, Anglicans, Baptists, Congregationalists, Plymouth Brethren and members of the Religious Society of Friends.

He read modern languages at Glasgow and theology at Oxford; has held pastorates at Blockley in the Cotswolds and in London at Westbourne Park (Paddington); in 1971 he became minister of College Street Baptist Church, Northampton, where he is also Free Church chaplain to St. Crispin and Princess Marina psychiatric hospitals.

Since 1962 he has worked on and off for *The Baptist Times* as a columnist and feature writer; has devised and directed acts of celebration and worship for the English Baptist Union, the Baptist Missionary Society, and the European Baptist Federation; he was for six years chairman of RADIUS, the Religious Drama Society of Great Britain.

Currently he is a part time research student under David Millar at Glasgow University's department of practical theology.

Beginning

a. to church with a purpose

1

On Sunday

'Observe the Sabbath and keep it holy.'   Exod 20:8

O God we thank you
for setting your day apart
as holy
       – not holy as though other days were profane,
         but holy so as to teach us that all time
         is a sacred trust from you.

We thank you
for the fellowship and business of your house today.
We thank you for allowing us to share
in the ministry of prayer and witness.

Forgive all our past sins, all our failures to love,
      to imagine, to serve and to help.
Forgive us for words said in haste and unkindly,
      and for our silence when we should have spoken.

Touch now with your Spirit
the offering of worship which we try to bring.

By your grace make it something to glorify you and
    bless us.

Let there be healing here,
encouragement, cheer and truth
in Christ's name.

2

In Church

'. . . Jesus . . . went as usual to the synagogue.'   Lk 4:16

Gratefully we come into the peacefulness of this church.
Many of us, looking around, recognise friends;
the familiar pew is reassuring if not very comfortable;
we are used to the music,
and well remembered words recall us to a simpler faith
than is easy to hold, always, on a weekday.

Here we seek and sometimes find
that which deeply calms and feeds us:
sin is forgiven, anxiety becomes prayer,
You love us, Jesus proves it;
we have untroubled joy.

Flowers, people, carpet, polished wood,
and the memory of thousands here before us, many
    years . . .
It is good, Lord, to be here.
You are here.

We are the more grateful, because we know we cannot
    stay.
Like the others, and the others in other times,
we must go out again after worship:
work waits to be done, there are problems to be faced,
struggles to be fought, burdens and hurts to be borne.

Make this an armoury, O God, as well as a sanctuary,
a place for the sharpening of swords and wits;
a place we enter with joy

but leave with a joy that is stronger;
a place where wounds are bound up
so that your soldiers may return to the battlefield.

Help us by your grace to find and reinforce here
a peace which can persist outside, a sanctuary peace
which needs nó sanctuary;
so that we may have peace to share
with those who will not know peace unless they see it in
    us.

Forgive and understand our faltering words,
and answer our hearts' prayer
for the renewal of our life
in Jesus Christ our Lord.

3

For Worship
A responsive prayer

'to God be glory in the church . . .'   Eph 3:21

O God:
we are here/ TO GIVE YOU GLORY.

Because you love the world so much
that You sent Jesus Christ to be our Saviour,
O God:
we are here/ TO GIVE YOU GLORY.

Because a new and better way of living
is open to all who believe in Jesus your Son,
O God:
we are here/ TO GIVE YOU GLORY.

4

For Help
At a family service

'. . . the habit of meeting together . . .'   Heb 10:25

O God our heavenly Father:
we are here in your house for all sorts of reasons.
There's curiosity, there's habit –
and of course there's love of you,
because some of us are in touch with you already
in the friendship of Jesus Christ.
But, as we stop to think about it, there is one big reason
for being here:
we all need your help.

★

We need your help
if we are to lead good, honest, moral lives:
by ourselves we stumble and fall and lose the way.
We do what we know is wrong and say what we know
        is unkind,
and it is hard to tell the truth even when we know it.
So the first thing we need is your forgiveness,
and then your help to go straight.
We believe you will forgive and help –
because Jesus says so.

★

Therefore it is in Jesus' name that we come.
For his sake, please give us the pardon and peace,
and the power for living,
that we know we need.
Please listen to our prayers
for the people we care about and the world we live in,
because we want your help for everybody,
not just for ourselves.

★

Accept our worship,
forgive our sins,
bless the people we pray for,
and bless us too,
for Jesus' sake.

5

At a Family Service
After a trinitarian hymn such as "Holy, holy,
holy. . . ."

'. . . the Father, from whom every family in heaven and on earth
receives its true name . . .'   Eph 3:14–15

God our heavenly Father:
thank you for making us part of your family.
You sent your Son to be our friend,
to teach us that the world is a place you love,
and to make it up with You for all that we do wrong.
Thank you for his life of kindness
and his words of truth;
thank you for his death, when he never stopped loving
    us,
and for his risen life now,
in your heaven
and in our hearts.

★

You sent us your Holy Spirit, as Jesus promised you
    would.
He is like a wind that blows your Church along,
He is like a fire to give light and warmth and power,
He is like a dove,
    bringing messages and instructions to the Church.
He is the love and understanding
    that unites you and Jesus,
        come alive and lively into our lives.

★

O God, it is so exciting to be part of your family:
brothers and sisters of your Son,
servants of your Spirit,
children of your love.

★

O God, we are your family.
Please help us to be a credit to you;
forgive us when we grieve you and let you down;
help us to grow more and more like you
until in heaven we see you
and live joyfully for ever in your house.

★

Through Jesus Christ your Son,
who taught us to pray:

OUR FATHER. . . .

6

Royal Salute
At a parade service with the **Boys' Brigade

'Yes, Your Majesty . . . We are ready . . .'   2 Sam 15:15

Almighty God:
You are Father and King of us all.
We offer to you in worship
the salute which it is your right to receive
    and our duty to give.
From the oldest officer to the youngest boy in the
    Brigade,
and we who are parents and friends of the company
    (ies),
we are all united
in wanting to sing your praise
and honour your name.

(**for adaptation as appropriate to other organisations)

★

We admit that we are not worthy to serve you.
We have all sinned and come short
of the standard you set for human life
in the character of Jesus Christ your Son.

★

Yet we claim the friendship which he has held out to us,
we ask for the pardon which he secured
by his life, death and rising.
For his sake, please forgive our sins.
For his sake, please let us help
with the work of your kingdom,
amongst boys and amongst everyone else as well.

★

For his sake, please lead us on in Christian living,
to greater knowledge, deeper understanding, better
        service,
truer love for you and our fellow men.
For his sake hear our prayer,
as we sum it up in words he gave us:

OUR FATHER. . . .

7

Reminders
Prayer of approach to Communion

'Do this in memory of me.'   Lk 22:19

AWARENESS   O God, there is so much here
                to remind us of your presence.
                Around this building there gather
                other people's memories,
                and our own,
                of worship and prayer in time past.

The sight and scent of flowers
given for your house and arranged for
  your glory;
the music and the hymns,
the words of scripture and prayer;
and on the table the holiest reminders
  of all –
bread, of which Jesus said, 'This is my
  body',
wine, of which Jesus said, 'This is my
  blood'.
O God, we thank you for your
  nearness,
and for your mercy toward us
established and made clear
in Jesus Christ our Lord.

CONFESSION But, Father in heaven, who are we
to have such a privilege –
to meet in your presence and celebrate
  your love
– we who have sinned?
Father, forgive our sins
of thought, word and deed,
the faults we have forgotten,
and the wrongness which is so much
  part of us
that we are not aware of it.
Grant us the mercy promised to us in
  Christ,
and by your Spirit in the inner man
remake us in his likeness.

PEACE & JOY So may there be glory for you
in us;
and in us there can be peace
since we shall know that we have peace
  with you;
so may our joy be full, as Jesus said,
– for we pray in his name.

8

Undeserved Access
Approach to Communion, after the hymn
'Blest are the pure in heart . . .'

'. . . they will see God!'   Mt 5:8

Confession
O God our Father, we confess
that we do not have the purity of heart
which deserves to see you.
Even at our best
we lack the single-minded dedication
to knowing truth, loving people, and doing good,
of those who hunger and thirst after righteousness.
– and we are not often at our best.
We desire what is wrong, we admire what is
    second-rate,
we say what is unkind and we do what is dishonest.
We are even proud of ourselves
for being clever, sophisticated, worldly-wise.
It is not as though we could claim, most of us,
that our sins are very interesting –
we must bore you as often as we offend you.
O God, we are simply not fit for your company.

★

Yet here is where we want to be, here in your presence.
We want the gift that is offered to the pure in heart:
we need to know you.

★

Thank you, heavenly Father,
for promising the gift we do not deserve.
Thank you for your pardon.
Thank you for accepting on our behalf
the purity of heart that is in Jesus Christ your Son.
For his sake receive us now;

Forgive and blot out our sin and unworthiness;
clothe us in *his* purity.
Fill us with the joy and power of living as your children.

9

Thanksgiving

'. . . always . . . with a thankful heart.'   Phil 4:6

Father, we thank you for another week of life
in the world you made for your children to live in.
Thank you for work and the strength to do it,
for friends and loved ones and leisure to be with them.
We thank you for the times we have been happy,
the times we have been thoughtful,
and the times when we have laughed.
We thank you for hunger and thirst, food and drink,
for gentle weariness at a day's end, and the sweetness
 of sleep.
Thank you for your gifts of patience and humour,
given to help us in the times which were not easy;
and for all the people
who said and did things which made a difference
and sent us on our way with renewed courage.

10

Approach

'Let us . . . approach God's throne, where there is grace.'   Heb 4:16

Draw near to us now, O God,
in the reading and preaching of your word,
By your Holy Spirit help us in the ministry of prayer.
Grant us your peace, to have and to share,
and when, in obedience to your Son's command,
we break bread together,
sustain us with his life.

b. thanks, praise & joy

11

So Far, so Good

'The Lord has helped us all the way . . .'   1 Sam 7:12

Heavenly Father:
we lift up our hearts to praise you in Jesus' name,
depending on your gracious Holy Spirit
to guide our thought
and make up the imperfection of our worship.

★

We thank you
for bringing us safely to this day and place,
not too much hurt and not too much discouraged
by the ups and downs of another week.
We thank you for all the victories that have been won:
the kind words spoken,
especially when it would have been easier
and quite natural to be cross;
for the work well done,
and the friendships kept in good repair.
We thank you for all the times
when you have made us wiser,
                              wittier,
                              more patient and cheerful
                              than we might have been.

★

We thank you
for all the ways in which our lives have been sustained
by other people: people whose business yields

our food,
our clothes,
our light and heat
and our safety.
We thank you for firm friends, dependable colleagues,
the fellowship of the Church,
and for all the love, joy and variety of our home life.

★

Forgive us for our failures and sins.
By your pardon give us peace with the past;
by your grace give us strength for the future.

★

Take into your wise hands
the things and people that cause us anxiety.
We bring to you the worry which comes from fear
                    and the worry which comes from love;
we bring them as a burden which we must lay down,
and a prayer which you will take up
through Jesus Christ our Lord.

12

He is Faithful

'. . . we can trust God to keep his promise.' Heb 10:23

O God, we give you glory
for your faithfulness:
we thank you for the measured sequence of days,
the dependable return of the seasons,
and for the fruitfulness of soil and living things.
We thank you for the record of human trust in you
through the centuries,
and for the testimony we receive
that no-one who trusted you has ever been forsaken.

★

Look in mercy upon us now
as we worship you.
Forgive our sins.
Renew our strength.
Deepen our faith
and make our faith more obedient
                    and practical,
                    so that piety may express itself
                    in action as well as word.

★

Listen to the intercessions of your Church
here and everywhere.
Through our prayers and in our lives
may your will be done on earth as it is in heaven,
and may the power and glory all be yours,
as Jesus your Son taught us to pray,
saying:

OUR FATHER. . . .

13

He is Generous

'The Lord blessed you in every way . . .'   Deut 28:47

Great God and Father:
we rejoice each day in your gifts –
so many things to sustain our life
and delight our spirit.
Food, clothing and shelter protect our bodies;
we have people to love, work to do and ambitions to live
        for.
You even put in our hearts the yearning
for truth and goodness, justice and peace,
and to our deepest and highest awareness

your word speaks
– answering our hope with your grace,
   answering our fear with your love.

★

We thank you for all your gifts,
but we do not want to set our hearts entirely
on what you give;
for what we need is you, the giver.
Gifts, even the highest and holiest gifts,
take their value from the love which gives them;
and what we most deeply need,
what, in the end of all counting, we live by,
is your love.

★

By your Holy Spirit, free our worship and us
from all idolatry;
make us free to love you, not because of what you give,
though we thank you for it;
free to love you, not because of the hell you spare us
or the heaven you promise us,
though we rejoice in glorious hope.
Graciously lead us to where we cannot come
in our own strength or virtue
– to the point of loving you
   with the purity of heart
   that shall see God.

★

This is not a thing for words,
even the words of prayer;
but as we wait for your help in worship,
and for the fire from your altar which can purge our lips,
we dare to speak the best words we know,
since your own Son gave them to us:

OUR FATHER. . . .

14
He is Good

'Your Father . . . knows what you need . . .'   Mt 6:8

O God, we thank you
for making life good and for teaching us
whom to thank for its goodness.

★

The flavour of food when we are hungry,
laughter of children and chatter of friends,
zest when day begins, and sweet weariness when day is
     done,
the challenge of work and the comfort of home,
books and ideas and arguments,
the sudden bright idea,
and the involuntary return of memory
– all these are gifts from a loving Father to his children
   and we rejoice in them.

★

We thank you too, for gifts that are bitter-sweet:
the changeability of the weather, and the shifting
     moods
of mind and spirit;
and the share we have of pain, sorrow, regret and
     tension,
so that we are made participants in the rough game of
     life,
not watchers merely,
and sympathy becomes not just a word but a fact.

★

We bless you for this day in your house:
the heritage of faith,
the example of the saints,
the truth of scripture,
the warmth of praise,

the tug of prayer,
the renewal of fellowship,
and the rekindled hope that we shall have eternal glory,
the recaptured sense that we live already with eternal
    life.

★

Your grace lifts us up
from guilt,
from the fear of death and from timidity in living;
your grace has given us a share
in the royalty of Christ.

★

We give you glory
for all good things made better
and all bad things made bearable
through him who is our life,
Jesus, your Son, our Lord and Saviour.

15

He is Great and Wise
After the hymn
'God is good: we come before him . . .'

'. . . the Lord . . . is good, . . . the greatest . . . by his wisdom he
made the heavens.'   Ps 136: 1, 2, 5

O God,
you are good: and we praise you for your goodness.
You have given us life and all that makes it worth living,
home, friends, work and daily bread,
all our joy in things of earth,
all our hope of joy in heaven.

O God,
you are great: and we praise you for your greatness.
You show your power in our creation,

and our salvation,
and supremely
in the resurrection of Jesus your Son,
the pledge of your power to save.

O God,
you are wise: and we praise you for your wisdom.
In your wisdom you waited for the fullness of time
when Jesus should come;
in your wisdom you knew
there was no other good enough
to pay the price of sin;
he only could unlock the gate of heaven
and let us in.

Almighty God our Father, good and great and wise:
                  we worship and adore you.
                  Your Spirit calls us to worship
                  and enables us to pray.
May the words of our lips and the thought of our hearts
be acceptable to you
in Jesus Christ.

(The hymn or a choral setting such as Eric Thiman's,
may alternatively follow the prayer.)

16

Love
After a hymn such as
'God is love: let heaven adore Him . . .'

'. . . God is love.'   1 Jn 4:8

We praise the love
which creates all things,
making the heavens magnificent
and the earth fair and fruitful.
We praise the love
which cherishes all that it has made,

still valuing even fallen man,
recalling, reclaiming, restoring the penitent
by complete forgiveness.

We praise your love,
O God whose name and nature is love,
for the victories of your love in the hearts of mankind.
We praise you for all the people,
already remade in the likeness of Jesus Christ your Son
and glorious with Him and the saints in heaven.

We praise you for the multitude of believers now on
    earth
who have not reached the heavenly glory,
but hope for it through faith
in Christ crucified and risen.

O God,
make us part of the great company in heaven and on
    earth
who praise You in tongues of angels and men.

By your presence with us
quicken our faith to believe
and toughen our wills to obey,
as your Word made flesh in Christ is proclaimed
through the power of his name,
the name in which we pray.

17

Joy

'You have given them great joy, Lord . . .'   Is 9:3

'To glorify you and enjoy you for ever' . . . not an idea
that we should have dared to invent for ourselves:
that sinful human souls should be destined
to *take pleasure* in *you*,
almighty, everlasting God, King of kings and Lord of
    lords!

Yet it is so; experience proves it;
enjoyment *is* in view.
The salute of worship which is our duty, is also our joy.
There is no exaltation of spirit
like that of being caught up in your praise,
no higher delight than to sing a mighty hymn,
or read aloud the words
of prophet's vision or apostle's testimony.
For us there is no glory like the glorifying of you.

★

Not only in high moments of ordered worship –
sometimes with friends at evening, among beauty in the
    hills,
there comes the peace which is your gift,
flooding mind and spirit
as we see at peace the good world you created,
and feel that we belong to it.
Then we glimpse what it means
to rest in the Lord. . . .
to dwell in the presence of our heavenly Father,
to be calm there, confident in a Companion
most holy, trusted, strong.

★

With joy we recognise you
in little, vital dependabilities.
Day dawns, and time which you invented keeps strict
    tempo;
seasons follow, after winter always spring,
autumn after summer.
Friends once made stay constant,
acquired skills remain with us,
a dropped stone falls, sparks fly upward.
The world in which we live makes sense
– the sense you give it.

★

Your promises come true.
Those who mourn are blessed with comfort;
peacemakers know your peace;
today's grace matches today's need
if tomorrow's variables are left out of the equation.
Trusting you,
the leaden-hearted
rise up with wings as eagles.

★

Your gift, your doing, this grace that bears us up,
the peace and joy and faith which last deep down in us
below the levels where happiness comes and goes
with chance and circumstance.
The centre of our life
is hidden with Christ in you, and *there* is *joy*
undeserved, undeservable, inexhaustible and complete,
the table laid in the midst of foes,
the rod and staff of sure help
in the death-dark valley.

★

We taste and see that the Lord is good, good to us.
Glory be to him who condescends,
as though it were no condescension,
to become our joy
in Christ our Saviour.

18

Hope

'. . . God, the source of hope . . .'   Rom 15:13

Lord God: every morning of our lives
you are already in the day to which we waken.
At your command the earth has rotated, orbited and
       moved
to the right position in the immensity of space,

which you put there for it to be in.
Creator and stage manager of universe and world,
you have set the scene:
sparkling frost, bright sun or clammy fog,
traffic noise muted by snow or hissing with rain,
birdsong out of doors or a sneeze in the next room,
all are your special effects
given to induce a certain tone,
establish a certain mood in which we can revel
or against which we must contend.

★

Into our future you advance ahead of us.
That is what makes the future bearable, inviting,
full of possible meaning.
Your presence in the future gives us hope.
For our life and the life of mankind you are preparing
something good –
not just a future which will happen,
but a future we can help to fashion
with you and for you.

★

Lord, lift up every heart
which began this day with too little hope.
If *we* haven't noticed you yet in today,
open our eyes to see.

★

In what we must do today, may we serve you.
In those we meet today, may we meet you.
In all who need us today, may we realise the
        opportunity
to love with love like yours in Christ.

Forgive the sins we repent of;
forgive the sins we have forgotten;
forgive the sin of which we are not even conscious.
Set us free into today's opportunities
with a clear conscience and a clear head.

★

Give us grace to see possibilities hidden in situations
we had thought difficult or intractable.
With people we now find hard to take, give us patience,
then sympathy, and finally the seeds of friendship.

★

Lord God,
the scripture says you make all things new.
Make all things new this day.
Give us such hope in you
that we become optimistic about everyone and
      everything else.
Lord of all hopefulness, Lord of the future,
lead us forward with a light step and a courageous
      heart;
to your honour and glory,
and for the sake of Jesus Christ,
your Son, our Saviour.

c. the need for pardon

19

Homecoming
At a Communion service

'I am no longer fit to be called your son.'   Lk 15:19, 21

Almighty and merciful Father:
You welcome us to your day,

to your house,
to the fellowship of your people,
to the communion of your table.

We do not in the least deserve your welcome
for we have sinned
in thought, word and action,
in leaving duties undone and opportunities
missed,
and in spoiling the life You have given.

Forgive us, Father,
and deepen in us the marvellous knowledge
that we *are* forgiven;
that you look at us who believe
as though we were wearing the virtue
of Jesus your Son;
that for his sake you accept us
as your family.

We depend on you not only for the forgiveness of our
sins
but even for strength to draw a breath or take a step,
and for grace to walk each day
in patience, hope and love.

Give us your Holy Spirit
so that we may worship you.
Give us your blessing
so that we may continue
faithful, trusting, obedient
through Jesus Christ
who teaches us to pray,
saying:

OUR FATHER. . . .

20

On Firm Ground

'. . . God . . . who does not change . . .'   Jas 1:17

Great God and Father:
amid the changes and chances of our mortal days
we turn our eyes by faith to you
who are the Unchanging One: undiminished in your
    power,
        unsullied in your holiness,
        constant in your love
        for those whom you have made.

We bring you our sins, so that you may forgive them;
we bring you our sense of failure
so that you may comfort us
and restore the confidence
of creatures whom you accept as your children,
                appoint as your heirs,
                and commission as your servants,
                        despite what we are.

We bring you our eyes
    which have been dazzled
    by things which glitter but are not gold;
we bring you our ears
    which have been deafened
    with ill news and daunting threats from the world
    around us.

Clear our vision with the sight of your glory;
strengthen our hold upon your word of truth.
Confirm us, by faith,
in that eternal life
which begins on earth
and shall continue for ever in heaven,
through the merits of Jesus Christ our Saviour.

21

Sunday Best
After the hymn 'Worship the Lord in the beauty . . .'

'Bow down . . . in garments of worship.'　Ps 96:9 (margin)

Lord God:
we want to worship you in the beauty of holiness,
but we cannot.
We find it easier to be clever than to be holy
– and we are not even very clever.
We find it easier to be busy than to be holy
– though we are not really as busy as we would like to
　　seem.

★

Father of Jesus and our Father:
You can see through all our pretences
and we want you to see through them.
For we believe you understand us
with a Father's understanding
and will forgive us with a Father's love.
We believe that, while you want us perfect
　　　　　　　　and while you work for our perfection,
yet you love us as we are,
because you see us as those for whom your own Son
　　died.

★

So we offer you ourselves and our worship
in Jesus Christ.
We worship you in the beauty of *his* holiness
since we have none of our own.
Receive us and help us
for his sake.

22

Construction

'But each one must be careful how he builds.'   1 Cor 3:10

Loving Father:
we cannot be sure
that our thoughts, intentions and actions during the
      past week
have borne good fruit,
or that what we have built is on firm foundations.
At best we can claim that we meant well,
some of the time. . . .
and for the rest, when we have not *deliberately*
lied, cheated or idled,
we may have sinned through folly, inattention or
      forgetfulness.

★

We can be sure only
of your grace,
of your love,
of your goodwill toward us.

★

So we ask your grace to make good what we have done
      badly;
we ask your love still to keep us in its grasp;
we ask your goodwill to forgive our sins
and to bring some blessing even out of our folly.

★

And for any good that we may have done,
any love you have enabled us to show,
we give you all the glory, for it is yours,
and we thank You for stooping to use us
in the doing of your will.

23

Our Need

'I thirst for you, the living God . . .'   Ps 42:2

Almighty God:
you have given us life,
the power to live and a world to live in.
You have given us the sense to recognise our need
for light and heat, for food and for one another.
You have given us wit and understanding,
with the ability to think and wish, love and yearn
and even to recognise, if only we will,
our need of you.

★

Forgive us that we use our life, our strength and our
        wits
so often to run away from you,
and so rarely to seek you.
We admit our need of lesser things,
we shout and struggle to get them;
but our need of you, on whom all else depends,
we so readily forget
or underrate.

★

Awaken us fully in this moment to our need of you,
give us the thirst for you of which the psalmists sang.
Stir us to fight like Jacob for your blessing,
humble us to sue for your pardon like David.

★

God our Father: forgive our sins,
                reinforce our virtue,
                deepen our love,
                revive our faith,
                reopen the eyes of our understanding
                and renew the springs of our life.

★

For this we have come to your earthly house;
and this we dare to claim
at the word and in the name of Him who said,
'Ask and you shall receive,
seek and you shall find'
– your Son our Saviour,
    Jesus Christ.

24

Our Folly

After the hymn 'Souls of men, why will ye scatter . . .'

'Fools say to themselves, "There is no God".'   Ps 14:1

O GOD, WE CONFESS THE FOLLY
WHICH KEEPS MANKIND FROM YOU.
    From the sound of your Gospel and the life of your
        Church
    men and women do scatter like frightened sheep
    – and you all the time their Shepherd!
    We confess it, remembering that we too have run
        away
    from your people and your Word,
    or come unwillingly
    – to Sunday School perhaps because we had to,
        to church from habit,
        from convention,
        or from a loyalty without love.
    We confess the folly which keeps men and women
        from you,
    we confess in the name of those we represent
    because we, their relatives and friends,
    could not persuade them to come with us.
    If in their folly they say
    that there is no God,
    or that if there is he is not worth taking notice of,
    or that if he exists and matters, it is still no use

listening to what the Church says about him. . . .
If so, forgive them, enlighten them,
and forgive us for failing
to teach them better.

O GOD, WE CONFESS THE FOLLY
WHICH SPOILS YOUR CHURCH.
Forgiven everything by you,
we are still slow to forgive each other;
saved by amazing grace, we are ungracious.
With minds set on things above
and treasure laid up in heaven,
we stoop to ambition and worldly greed.
Like the first disciples we see your providence today,
yet worry still about tomorrow.
The holy Church throughout all the world doth
idiotically persist in division, pride
and visible wealth.
The light has shone upon us
and we have the mind of Christ,
but we have to admit as he did
that the children of this world are often brighter
than the children of light.

GIVE WISDOM TO MANKIND:
that men and women may seek you,
hear you,
obey your commands which order joyful justice,
and receive your gift which is pardon and peace.

GIVE WISDOM TO YOUR CHURCH:
that with astonishment and relief
we may ourselves listen
to the message of forgiveness we are preaching.
Open us up to your Spirit
– your love, your joy, your power.

WE CAST OURSELVES ONCE MORE UPON YOUR
MERCY.
In our folly and sin you have still loved us.
You have still used us, despite our idiocy and evil.

Forgive us. In your great grace make us wise.
Enable us to do those greater things
which you intend shall yet be done
through Jesus Christ our Lord.

25

Good, Great, Wise
After the hymn 'God is good: we come before Him . . .'

'Praise the Lord, because he is good.'   Ps 135:3

Give to your servants, O God,
reverence for your goodness,
trust in your greatness,
and ears obediently open to your wisdom.

★

TO YOUR GOODNESS we bring our sins,
sins deliberate and unconscious,
sins of intention and of disposition,
sins we commit in anger, malice and wrong desire,
sins we commit by failing and forgetting
– all our lack of love and sympathy and care,
   all our taking of one another for granted,
   even when we receive from one another
   service rendered at great cost.
Holy Father, forgive us and grant us your peace.

★

TO YOUR GREATNESS we bring our fears.
The peace of our life feels threatened
by the possibility of becoming ill or poor,
by the fear of losing friends or making enemies.
The peace of our world feels threatened
by the remorseless ambition of other nations
and by the folly and weakness of our own;
by the existence of terrible weapons,

and the seeming shortage of patience, charity and
     imagination
among those who appear to wield most power.
   Renew and deepen our conviction
   that all things *are* in your hand,
   that you love the world and all your children in it,
   and that your gracious purposes for mankind
   will be fulfilled in time and in eternity.
Almighty God, King of kings and Lord of lords,
convince us of your kingdom, and grant us your peace.

★

TO YOUR WISDOM we bring our ignorance and
     foolishness –
so many things we do not understand:
how to be rich without pride, how to be poor without
     rancour;
how to be angry without sinning;
how to love without spoiling;
How to be impatient to do what must be done
while being patient to bear what must be borne.
Teach us, Father,
how to think, how to pray,
how to live and how to love, and grant us your peace.

★

Through Jesus Christ our Lord.

25(b)

Adaptation for three voices at a youth service

VOICE 1:
God, you are good;
and to your goodness we bring our sins
and our sorrow for them,
so that we may be forgiven.
Forgive the sins we commit on purpose,

dishonest words and spiteful actions.
Forgive the sins we commit by accident,
through not loving enough, through not thinking
      enough
and through taking other people too much for granted.
Heavenly Father, in your goodness
forgive us and make us good
as Jesus is.

VOICE 2:
God, you are great:
and to your greatness we bring our fears
and our need to be strengthened,
so that we may know your power.
The peace of our world seems threatened
by people who want to fight
and by the existence of terrible weapons.
Some of the people who wield great power
seem to be short of patience, imagination and kindness;
people who rule seem not to care.
Convince us, who believe in Jesus,
that you are going to get your way in the end,
and that love and goodness will win.
Great God, King of kings and Lord of lords,
give us a share in your victory,
and grant us your peace always,
as Jesus promised.

VOICE 3:
God, you are wise;
and to your wisdom we bring our ignorance and
      foolishness.
There are so many things we don't understand:
how to be fortunate and successful without becoming
      proud;
how to be unlucky without becoming resentful;
how to be angry without sinning;
how to love without spoiling;
how to be impatient to do what needs doing,
and at the same time patient

with what has to be put up with.
Teach us, wise Father,
how to pray and how to think,
how to live and how to love
as Jesus does.

ALL THREE:
O God, good, great and wise,
may we honour your goodness,
may we trust your power,
may we learn your wisdom –

VOICE 1:
through Jesus Christ our Saviour
who taught us all to pray:

    OUR FATHER. . . .

(All three lead the congregation in saying the Lord's
Prayer)

26

In the King's Presence

'. . . I compose this song for the king.'   Ps 45:1

King of kings and Lord of lords:
with heart and mind we offer you
the salute of our worship.
We believe you made the universe
and that you rule it.
We thank you for all the goodness
which we know and experience,
because you are its source.

We know
that despite your love and grace
much is wrong with your world,
and it does not seem very like your kingdom.

We confess our own imperfection and perversity,
and admit our share
in the evil around us.

★

In your presence
we can think of no goodness in ourselves
which we could bring to you
as a peace offering.
All the good we ever attempt
is dependent upon your grace.
We can only put ourselves once more
into the hands of your boundless mercy.

★

We ask you to forgive our sins,
and to grant us strength
so that we may live with loyal patience
as your subjects,
and play our part in bringing nearer
the day when all things and all people
shall own you as King.

27

Centre Point
After the hymn
'Let us with a gladsome mind . . .'

'. . . he is good; his love is eternal.'   Ps 136:1

Lord God:
we remember all that we have seen
of human goodness
– the courage of martyrs,
  the patience of saints,
  the sweetness of innocence,
  the power of righteousness,
and we remember

that everything we have ever admired in other people
is only a reflection, distant and faint,
of your holiness.
Here with you
we are at the source
and centre
of good
for you are holy.

★

Our bad conscience makes us afraid,
or it would do,
but for your gracious words
of invitation and welcome:
    'Come unto Me, all you who carry burdens',
    'Come, let us reason together, you with sins like
        scarlet'
    'Son, your sins are forgiven'.

★

Forgive us, for we have sinned;
receive us, for we have returned.
Restore to us the joy of your salvation,
and do not take your Spirit from us.
So may we continue to praise you with a gladsome
    mind,
for your enduring mercy and kindness
shown to us and all men
in Jesus Christ our Lord.

d. what we believe

28

Mighty Acts
After reading Psalm 111:2 or Psalm 66:3

'How wonderful are the things the Lord does!'   Ps 111:2

'How wonderful are the things the Lord does!'
Lord God, we hear the psalmist's words
and say 'Amen'.
Everything we call achievement
is dwarfed by what you do.

> We build houses, to have a roof over our heads,
> but then, you spread out the heavens above us.
> We study to acquire knowledge, and a few of us
>   become wise,
> but then, you gave man his brain, and it is you
> who guarantee the truth of what is true.
> Old men dream dreams, young men see visions;
> beauty, fear, love, time and death
> make poets of us all, we say,
> but then, it is your Holy Spirit
> who inspires all the seeing and singing,
> all the wondering and writing
> that men have ever done.

All man's making is with thought and things you give
    him,
and his making is done in the span of life you lend him.
All we do, you make us able to do.
And when thought and power lead us astray,
your wisdom still is greater than our folly
and can mend our foolishness;
your mercy still is greater than our sin,
and can renew us.

★

We offer you
the simple recognition
that you are God;
and the acknowledgment
that we are your creatures,
turning to you for what it takes
to live, to learn and to love
in this life
and in the life that is to come.

★

We seek your pardon
and your blessing
as Jesus taught us to do,
saying:

OUR FATHER. . . .

29

Kingdom Come
A Prayer of Obstinate Faith,
after the hymn: Jesus shall reign where'er the sun
Does his successful journeys run;
His Kingdom stretch from shore to
shore,
Till moons shall wax and wane no
more.'

'His kingdom will reach from sea to sea.'   Ps 72:8

Lord Jesus Christ:
forgive us if these are not the right words
in which to speak of your reign.
Perhaps they make the Kingdom sound too much
like a world in which *we* shall have it all our own way,
sharing your throne as some of your first disciples
dreamed of doing.

Perhaps our words say too much
about how *nice* everything will be for *us*
when you rule the world,
and not enough
about the terrible glare of your glory,
the justice of your administration,
or our *duty* to you.

★

So forgive us, Lord, if the words are wrong,
but after all our faith is not in words;
we do not believe in what we say about you –
we believe in you.
In you we glimpse the face of God your Father,
in you we grasp, though clumsily, at what is true
and real and good and eternal and *worth grasping*.
We believe in you,
and whatever it means we want you to rule
in heaven, on earth, in us.

★

We want you to have your way,
wherever it leads and whatever it costs.
Let us be your disciples,
your brothers and sisters in this world and the next.
To your own promise that this can happen
we cling with all the strength we have
and all the faith you give us.
Lord, we believe;
help our unbelief.

★

Forgive our half-belief and half-commitment,
the way we cling to things that are not you.
Teach us to seek and find and serve you only
– in trusty friend and needy neighbour,
   and in all the comings and goings of daily life.
Purge and transform our loves, ambitions, and hopes,
into aims that can be part of *your* aim.

★

So shall you be our King,
so shall you reign, to the blessing of God's people
and the glory of God's name.

30

On the First Day of any Week

'. . . in the Temple giving thanks to God.'   Lk 24:53

In Jesus' name we praise you, O God,
for it is in Jesus that we see you –
in him, without whom nothing was created,
in him, your love made visible,
in him whose sacrifice makes our peace with
you,
in him, your Word made flesh.
In Jesus' name we praise you for your Word of
CREATION
by which we and all else exist.

We praise you
for your Word of TRUTH on which depends the
certainty
of all that is certain:
all fact verifiable by science,
all noble thought by which a man may live,
all that is seemly in art or behaviour.

We praise you
for your Word of LOVE, steadfast and abiding,
by which we know
that you love your children
even when they have strayed into folly, sin and
defilement,
for you are slow to anger
and plenteous in mercy,
desiring not the death of a sinner
but rather that he should turn from his
wickedness and live.

We praise you
for your Word of PARDON in which stands all our hope
        of peace and heaven.
           'Father, forgive them' was Christ's prayer upon
                the cross,
           'Your sins are forgiven' was what he said with
                power to heal and restore,
           'Repent, be baptized, receive the Holy Spirit'
                was the gospel invitation
                to all who would believe.

For creation,
for truth,
for love,
for pardon we praise and thank you.

★

And we give you glory
for raising Jesus from the dead,
setting the seal of victory upon all he did and suffered,
and confirming the blessed hope
that we who believe in him may not perish
but have everlasting life.

31

Providence
After the hymn
'Father, I know that all my life
Is portioned out for me . . .'

'The days allotted to me had all been recorded in your book, before
any of them ever began.'   Ps 139:16

Father, I know. . . .
That is to say, Father, I more or less believe. . . .

Thank you, God, for hymn-writers
who can put into words for us what we believe,

or what we are supposed to believe,
or what we find it hard to believe
even when we know it is true.

Thank you for the truth in the hymn we have just sung:
that in all things you work together for good
with those who love you,
those whom you have called to faith in Jesus Christ.

Once again we commit ourselves to believing it.
Thank you for the things which help us to believe it:
      the things you allowed to happen to us,
      the friends you led us to make,
      the lessons you caused us to learn
      in readiness for a time when we would
         need to have learned them.
      Looking back we begin to see a pattern,
      or part of what might be a pattern,
      and sometimes we can say,
      'Hitherto hath the Lord helped'.

Forgive us, Father, that it is only sometimes.
Like Jesus' first disciples we forget old miracles
in the face of new problems.
We know you fed us yesterday,
but it is today that we feel hungry;
we know you led us yesterday,
but today we are lost again.
O teach us to trust you better.

In your presence now
we recall the things we were worrying about
before we came to church –
the state of the nation,
the value of the pound in our pocket,
the level of unemployment and the rate of growth if
    any;
the condition of our property or the size of our rent,
the health of the family,
problems waiting for us at work this week.

We cannot conceal these things from you,
or pretend they don't intrude upon our thoughts
this very minute.
You know our thoughts.
You know our worries,
and you know the measure of freedom from worry
which we have let you give us –
the measure of faith and hope and cheerfulness.
We thank you for that.
But what remains of the burden, this we bring to you
      now
in muddled prayer.

For our prayer *is* muddled.
Whatever our strength and confidence,
we are also partly weak, fearful and defeated.
However worried we are,
your grace has already begun its strengthening work.
Continue it, Father, your work of grace in us;
warm us with your love, convince us of your victory,
speed us on our way with words of cheer;
God help us.

Greater people, holier saints than we are, have prayed
      so.
To need you is not weakness, it is the only way to live.
Without you we can do nothing;
with you in Christ all things become possible.

So pleading turns to praise: you are such a God!
– exalting the humble and meek,
   using the weak to confound the mighty,
   the foolish to confound the wise.
Yours is the power of Christ's resurrection
and power for every resurrection of the human spirit.
We praise you, O God;
we acknowledge you to be the Lord.

'Family Church'

a. all together

1
Together

'All the believers continued together . . .' Acts 2:44

Here we are, heavenly Father,
meeting in your house on earth
which we call a church.
Some of us are very young,
some of us are quite old,
and we are all different.

Some of us are sad, some not very well,
some of us have a lot to worry about;
and we have come to ask for your help.
Some of us are very happy
and we have come to thank you
for our happiness.

But in some things we are all alike:
we all need to say sorry for the things we have done
    wrong;

we all want to offer you the things we have tried to do
　　　well;
we all want to say thank you for our lives,
and for all the good things you have done for us.

Above all,
every one of us needs to thank you
for sending Jesus
to be our Friend, our Teacher and our Saviour.

Hear us now,
as we say together
the prayer he taught us:
　　　OUR FATHER. . . .

2

Why we are Here

'I am the way, the truth, and the life . . .'　Jn 14:6

Heavenly Father:
we are here because of the most wonderful thing
you ever did –
because You gave Jesus Christ your Son
to be our revelation of your truth,
　　　our Saviour from sin,
　　　and our way back to you.
Thank you for Jesus.
The way he lived teaches us what you are like;
his death shows how completely you love us;
his resurrection convinces us
　　　of your power over death,
　　　and of your intention to raise us to everlasting life;
his presence day by day with us who trust him
　　　gives purpose and strength to our living.

★

O God, you have created us,
you keep us alive and help us to enjoy living;

each breath of air, each bite of food,
each gesture of friendship, kindness or love
is a gift from you.

★

And above all
You have called us through Jesus
into the life of your family
and the service of your kingdom.

★

Father, forgive us
for showing so little interest in your call,
so little response to your love,
so little sign of growing more like Jesus.
Forgive us all our sins.
Use this time of worship now
to bring us another step nearer to you.
Convince us that our sins *are* forgiven.
Help us to hear your Word with understanding and
    obedience.
Renew our strength.
Deepen our fellowship with one another
and with you in Jesus Christ.

★

Fill us with the joy of belonging
to your family,
as we say:

    OUR FATHER. . . .

3

Celebration
A Prayer for Leader and Children to say line by line

'. . . always be joyful in . . . the Lord.'   Phil 4:4

Lord God, we praise you.
We are happy to be here.
We thank you that we are alive:
we have not starved,
nor drowned, nor frozen,
nor been run over.

It can't be because we deserve it;
because we *don't* deserve it –
> we have thought wrong, said wrong, done
> wrong,
> so it must be *in spite of that* that you love us;
> You protect us and help us in spite of that.

Thank you, God, for your wonderful love
which treats us better than we deserve.

So we are glad to be here,
glad to be together,
glad to be together with you
in your house
amongst your people,
surrounded by your Spirit.

Help us to praise you,
help us to learn about you,
help us to pray,
help us to grow as Jesus grew
in wisdom as well as in years.
Help us to CELEBRATE the NEW LIFE that is ours
through Jesus Christ our Lord.

4

The Saviour
A prayer for Leader and Children to say line by line

'In all the world there is no one else . . . who can save us.'   Acts 4:12

God our heavenly Father and King:
we praise and thank you,
we who are older and we who are younger,
we who teach and we who are taught,
we praise and thank you
for our lives
and all our enjoyment of living.
Above all we thank you
for giving us Jesus your Son
to be our Saviour and Friend.
We thank you that he was born as we were
and grew up as we do.
We thank you that he showed us
the truth of your love and forgiveness,
and opened to us
the gate of everlasting life.
Help us to accept what he gives,
help us to trust him and love him,
help us to grow up in him,
for his name's sake.

b. Thank You, God

5

Happiness
A prayer for Leader and Children to say line by line

'Every good gift . . . comes from heaven.'   Jas 1:17

Thank you, God,
for all the things which make us happy:
feeling better after a cold,
feeling cosy at tea-time on chilly days,
having our favourite lesson at school,
being with our friends,
laughing at something funny,
managing to do something difficult,
knowing that you love us –
> for this above all we thank you;
> because being loved by you
> is happiness
> which nothing can ever take away:
> knowing you as our heavenly Father
> through Jesus Christ your Son.

6

Variety
A Prayer for Leader and Children to say line by line

'. . . gathered together in one place.'   Acts 2:1

O God our Father:
here we are, your family the Church.
We are all ages, some older, some younger;
we do different things,
we like different things,

we worry about different things.
But for the moment we are all together
doing the same thing.

We are thinking about you,
and remembering that you are our Father
and our God.
We remember that you gave your Son Jesus
to teach us about you,
and to put us in touch with you.
We ask you to forgive all our sins for his sake,
we ask you to help us live the way he taught,
we ask you to help us love one another
as you love us, in him.

Help us worship now:
help us to pray,
help us to listen,
help us to understand,
help us to rejoice together
in Jesus Christ our Lord.

7

Sensible Thanksgiving

'. . . be thankful in all circumstances.'   1 Thes 5:18

Lord God, keep us thankful.
Not just for the sake of being polite to you,
but for our own sake:
it will make us so much happier.
We don't want to be silly and pretend
that everything is good and lovely all the time:
plenty of things go wrong,
and plenty of things hurt and worry us;
and there are always our sins to be sorry for.
But the fact remains
that you give us many good things,
and that you bless us in many ways.

Help us always to remember this,
help us to rejoice in our hearts
whatever happens,
and so to shine with joy for you
through Jesus Christ our Lord.

8

Reading and listening

'You have the words that give eternal life.'   Jn 6:68

Thank you, God, for words.

Thank you for kind words
like 'dear' and 'please' and 'thankyou'.
Thank you for exciting words
in stories and songs.
Thank you for strong and helpful words
like 'hold tight' and 'this won't hurt much'
and 'of course you can'.

Thank you for the strong true words
which Jesus spoke about you:
about your love,
about your forgiveness of our sins,
and about eternal life
now and in heaven.

Thank you, God, for all the words
that come from you.
Please help us to feed upon them
as Jesus said we should.

9

All Sorts

'. . . he created all races of mankind . . .'   Acts 17:26

Thank you, Father in heaven,
for making us part of your earthly family,
the human race.
Thank you for giving us brothers and sisters
of all kinds and colours.
Thank you, too,
for making us part of your family the Church.
However old we are and however young,
however bright and clever we are, or aren't,
may we grow in love for you
and appreciation of one another,
today and always,
through the grace of Jesus Christ.

10

Togetherness and Difference

'. . . from every race, tribe, nation and language . . .'   Rev 7:9

Heavenly Father,
everybody's heavenly Father:
thank you for making so many different kinds of people
– yellow people with almond-shaped eyes,
   black people with crinkly hair,
   pink people with hair that's straight or wavy;
we speak different languages,
sing different songs,
dance differently, walk differently,
and we like different things to eat.

Since we are all so different,
we ought never to get bored with each other.
Thank you, Father, for making humanity
so interesting.

And Father, forgive us
if we have ever laughed at someone for being different,
or been unkind to someone because they were different,
or been afraid of someone because they were different.
Help us to remember always
that we all belong together
in your human family.

Help us to learn the lessons of love
taught by Jesus Christ your Jewish Son,
who is such a wonderful friend
to foreigners like us.

11

During a Dialogue Service

'Each one should firmly make up his own mind.'   Rom 14:5

Lord God our Father:
thank you for making us so different
in our ways of looking at things.

★

Teach us how to go on loving
across all our differences
of age, taste and opinion.

★

Keep us friends even when we argue –
may we become better and better friends
just because we *do* argue
– through the grace of our most patient Master and
    Saviour
Jesus Christ your Son.

12

At the Close of a Service
A Prayer for Leader and Children to say line by line

'. . . come in and go out and find pasture.'   Jn 10:9

Thank you, God, for home
and all the people who live there,
especially our parents.
Thank you for church
and all the people we meet there,
especially our teachers.
Thank you for Jesus
who has promised to be with his friends
always and everywhere.
Heavenly Father, bless our homes,
and protect us on our journey back to them,
for Jesus Christ's sake.

c. living thanks

13

Breadth

'God loved the world so much . . .'   Jn 3:16

O God our Father:
your love is big enough
to embrace the whole world.
Make our love big enough
to include all the people we meet,
even when they are different from us.
We ask this for Jesus' sake.

14

Limitation

'. . . my power is strongest when you are weak.'   2 Cor 12:9

Creator and Father of us all
in all our diversity:
we offer ourselves to You now
with all our shortcomings –

> the limitation of being young,
> the limitation of being old,
> the limitation of being
>   not exactly either.

We offer ourselves to you and to one another
so that we may find and serve one another's need,
and so that, as we do so,
we may find you
and serve you
in Jesus Christ your Son, our Lord.

15

Experience

'Find out for yourself how good the Lord is.'   Ps 34:8

Heavenly Father: we thank you
for all that we have come to know of your love
in Jesus Christ.
We thank you
for our experience of Jesus
as alive and present
in our daily life.

Help us to understand our experience,
and help us to recognise the times and places
at which it is right to speak of it.

Give us courage
to tell other people about Christ,
and give us wit
so as not to bore them
by the way we do it.

Give us grace to live genuinely Christian lives,
so that what we are
may not shout down what we say.

We commend to your blessing
all those teachers, preachers and missionaries
who are called to a life of full time evangelism.

But, Lord God,
help us not to leave it all to them,
for Jesus' sake.

16

Advertisement

'. . . your way of life should be as the gospel of Christ
requires . . .'   Phil 1:27

Thank you, heavenly Father,
for the good news of your love.
Thank you for the good news that sins can be forgiven,
and sinners turned into saints.
Thank you for the good news
that the friends of Jesus begin to live with a new sort of
    life,
the life that goes on for ever in heaven,
eternal life, full of joy and truth, kindness and love.

Thank you for all the people who tell the good news,
and thank you even more for those among them
whose lives demonstrate that the good news is true.

Please help us all to be good advertisements
for what we say we believe,
through Jesus Christ our Lord.

17

Time

'Everything . . . happens at the time God chooses.'   Ecc 3:1

Thank you, God, for time:
these days and hours and minutes
that you give to us.
Help us,
whether we are very young,
or somewhere in the middle of our journey through the
    days,
or really quite old –
help us not to waste a moment.

★

Let us not waste time in idleness when we should be
    busy;
let us not waste in feverish activity
time which we should use for rest.

★

Help us to catch each enjoyment
and savour it to the full;
help us to grasp each truth,
        cherish each friendship;
help us to use each opportunity
        for doing worthwhile things,
        for bravely putting up with pain or sorrow,
        for being still and knowing that you are God.

★

By your forgiveness
set us free from regret for the past.
By your grace help us to live in the present
    and live thoroughly.
By the hope which Jesus Christ your Son puts in our
    hearts,

enable us to travel cheerfully on
into the future
where you are sure to meet us.

18

After Congregational Discussion

'. . . many people had gathered and were praying.'   Acts 12:12

O God our heavenly Father:
    you have made everything and everyone,
    and what you make, you love.
When things go wrong you have the power
    to mend and heal.
In your creative love we ask you to mend and heal
    the people and things we have talked about.
    Give health
    and peace
    and food,
    give patience
    and wisdom
    and strength
      where they are needed.
And for ourselves. . . .
teach us to live like your friends and helpers,
      working with you to make things better
      and people happier,
      through Jesus Christ our Lord.

19

About the Church

'. . . We . . . are citizens of heaven . . .'   Phil 3:20

God our Father:
we pray for this church where we are,
and for all your Church,

in all its denominations,
in our district, in our country, in the world.

★

We know that churches are supposed to love Jesus,
and to love people the same way as he does.
We know that churches are supposed to honour you,
and to be colonies of your empire,
outposts of your kingdom.
We know that churches are supposed to be on fire
with the life and light and power
of the Holy Spirit.

★

O God, make all churches just like that,
ours too,
for Jesus' sake.

d. the Lord Jesus

20

Palm Sunday: a Prayer of Allegiance

'Look, your king is coming to you! He is humble and rides on a
donkey . . .'   Mt 21:5

King Jesus:
on this day
when you offer to our imagination
a picture of your kingship and your style of
        government,
we offer back to you our royal salute
of praise and allegiance.

★

Thank you, your Majesty,
for coming amongst us
as one who serves.

★

Royal Jesus:
teach us how to rule in your way
over those small kingdoms where we hold a little power
– at home,
   in school and at work,
   in the frames of reference,
   and the circles of friends,
   where we seem to matter.

★

Give us grace to make *our* royalty
a royalty of service and respect,
and *our* leadership
a leadership like yours
which does not subdue those who are led,
but ennobles them.

★

King Jesus, help us to be citizens
of your kingdom
for your name's sake.

21

Illumination

'. . . the light that . . . shines on all mankind.'   Jn 1:9

Lord Jesus:
light up our thoughts with your truth,
light up our lives with your beauty,
light up our homes with your love,
so that we may shine for you
always.

22

Believing

'. . . that through your faith in him you may have life.'   Jn 20:31

Lord Jesus Christ: we believe
that you are the most important Person
who has ever walked this earth.
We believe that you were there
when the earth was being created;
and that much later, though still a long time ago,
you lived a real human life,
died a real human death,
and came back to life again.

We believe that these are the facts,
and that holding on to these facts
changes the whole look of our life,
       our death,
       and our eternity.

Lord, we believe . . . well, we *say* we do.
Lord, make us absolutely
    and obstinately
    and infectiously
    CERTAIN about you.

Then you can do something with us
to transform the world
for everyone else.

23

Shining

'You are . . . light for the whole world.'   Mt 5:14

Lord Jesus:
you say that your friends are the light of the world.
Help us to light up our home,
    our school,
    our friendships
    and our work,

by shining with your sort of goodness,
                your sort of kindness
                and your sort of joy, truth and love.

24
Reacting

'. . . do not let your anger lead you into sin . . .'   Eph 4:26

Lord Jesus Christ:
when we find ourselves up against what we know is
    wrong

– in ourselves,
  in other people,
  in our nation
  or in the world –

please show us the RIGHT way to put it right,
and save us from lashing out and only making matters
    worse.

Help us to do the RIGHT thing,
and to do it YOUR way.

e. think, then pray

25
Surprise, surprise!

'. . . the crowd was amazed at the way he taught.'   Mt 7:28

*After talking to younger children about the word
'serendipity' which is likely to intrigue them;
or after introducing those slightly older to the*

phrase 'surprised by joy' which C. S. Lewis lifted
from a Wordsworth sonnet for his spiritual
　　autobiography.

★

Thank you, Lord Jesus,
for all our happiness.
Thank you especially
for the happiness which takes us by surprise.
Above all we ask you
to lead us toward the surprising discovery
that what most pleases you
will bring the greatest joy to us.

26

Political Awareness
After some sad thinking
on Remembrance Sunday
(a responsive prayer)

'Happy are those who work for peace . . .'   Mt 5:9

For people who are afraid
because fighting is going on around them
LORD GOD, HEAR US/
　　　　　　　　　WHEN WE PRAY IN JESUS'
　　　　　　　　　NAME.

For people who are trying to make peace,
some of them risking their own safety to do so,
LORD GOD, HEAR US/
　　　　　　　　　WHEN WE PRAY IN JESUS'
　　　　　　　　　NAME.

For people who are sad, because friends and relations
have died in war
LORD GOD, HEAR US/
　　　　　　　　　WHEN WE PRAY IN JESUS'
　　　　　　　　　NAME.

For people who find it all too easy to remember
and all too hard to forgive
LORD GOD, HEAR US/
                    WHEN WE PRAY IN JESUS'
                    NAME.

For ourselves, that we may be peacemakers,
and good neighbours to the rest of the world
LORD GOD, HEAR US/
                    WHEN WE PRAY IN JESUS'
                    NAME.

27

Lord, thank you
Responsive Prayer, with silence for thinking in

'You hear my voice in the morning . . .'   Ps 5:3

LET US THINK about breakfast:
                    about the people who got it for us,
                    or the people we got it for
                    – either way, the day began with
                        sharing.
                    Or if we began the day by ourselves
                    because we live by ourselves,
                    let's remember the things and people
                    we thought of when first we awoke
                    – especially the people;
                        because caring about them helps us
                        not to be lonely, even when we are
                        alone.

                    (pause for thought)

LORD/ THANK YOU.

LET US THINK about holidays; week-ends – *this*
                    week-end.

How pleasant to take a break, have a
        change.
Today, its opportunities;
the people we are with now, and the
        ones
we look forward to meeting later,
when we go out for a meal –
or friends who are coming to see us.
What a good thing life isn't all work!
What a good thing God evidently
        intends us
to relax as well as to concentrate
– he even means us to laugh!

(pause for thought)

LORD/ THANK YOU.

LET US THINK with regret, about the things
        which, quite frankly, we'd rather forget
        – our sins, and the qualities in us
            which even we don't admire;
        the snappish things we say sometimes,
        the old resentments we cling to;
        our selfishness,
        and the way we take people for granted,
        even people who matter to us a great
            deal.

(pause for thought)

LORD/ FORGIVE US.

LET US THINK about being helped; and about needing
            help;
        help to make a go of our job, our
            studies,
        our friendships and our faith;
        help to face the things which annoy us,
        and frighten us, and tempt us;
        help to live day by day
        like real disciples of Jesus Christ.

★

Only Jesus himself
can give us that sort of help;
but he will give it.
He has *promised* to give it
to everyone who asks him.

(pause for thought)

LORD/ HELP US.

28

Worship
After the senior choir has sung
Mendelssohn's anthem 'Above all praise and majesty'

'Sing psalms, hymns, and sacred songs . . .'   Col 3:16

THOUGHT

Yes, God is '*above* all praise and majesty'. He doesn't
   need praise
as we do, to bolster up his confidence or tell him he is as
   good
as he hopes he is.
Our worship surely can't *give* God anything. It would be
   as silly
to suppose that a fifty pence postal order on his birthday
would make your millionaire uncle feel richer.
Worship can seem silly in other ways too.
It can have the silliness of people who say they're not
   going to
do something, and then do it. . . .
'I don't want to sound rude', they say, and then they *are*
   rude;
'I don't want to seem greedy', then they eat a third
   helping;
'I don't want to bore you', when they know they will.

Just so, in worship we begin by saying something like,
'O God, I am not worthy to open my mouth in your
      presence',
and then carry on opening it for an hour or more.

★

Now for something astonishing.
The Bible and the Church are full of people quite
      convinced
that worship is not silly at all;
convinced that even when our worship sounds foolish,
God makes sense of it,
that even though our worship can add nothing to God's
      glory,
he seems to value it as if it could
– when we mean it, that is, when we really love him.

★

Perhaps it is a bit like the way your parents
appreciate the Christmas present you give them,
even when you bought it with pocket money they gave
      to you
in the first place. It is not silly;
the loving and the giving and the joy in receiving
are *real*.

★

Worship matters to God
not for being expensive or clever or beautiful
or pious or loud,
but for being *real*.
God really cares about us,
so when we really care about him
real worship happens, worship which Jesus called
worship 'in spirit and in truth'.

PRAYER

(for Leader and Children to say line by line)

Thank you, Lord God,
for letting us praise you;
because we enjoy doing it.
Thank you for listening
when we sing choruses and hymns and anthems.
Help us to mean what we say when we pray;
and as we enjoy singing your praises,
help us to live to your glory,
by living and loving
the way Jesus shows.
In his name we ask it.

29

God Cares
After reading Luke 12:22–30

'. . . I tell you not to worry . . .'   Lk 12:22

THOUGHT: CROWS AND CROCUSES

Have you ever seen a worried crow? Have you ever seen
a worried crocus? Jesus hadn't. And he noticed that the
crocus didn't go short of coloured petals, nor the crow
short of black feathers, for lack of worrying. So he
reckoned that worrying didn't help. Now take people, he
said: do anxious people live longer than calm people? No.
Well then, worrying doesn't help crows, or crocuses, or
people.

What's more, Jesus went on to argue something even
more interesting. Somebody cares about the crow – to
make sure he has feathers; somebody cares about the
crocus – to make sure she has a pretty dress of petals.
Then it is fair to assume that somebody cares about
people – to make sure there is daylight and food and air
and clothes for them. And Jesus was quite sure who the
Somebody is: God, our heavenly Father, as Jesus loved to
call him. So we don't need to worry.

We do need to work, of course. That's in the scheme of
things. Crows catch insects and peck seeds to get their

share of God's provision. Crocuses extract food from the soil and energy from the sunshine to get their share. So to get ours, we need to work, think, save, use hands and brains.

But what we don't need to do is worry.

In fact, worrying is really rather rude to God; like saying: Almighty God, are you SURE you haven't FORGOTTEN me?

★★★

PRAYER: Great God our Father, you do many
things:
the stars shine
and the sun warms the earth,
mountains are formed
and weather is organised;
the world spins,
tides heave,
the nations rise and fall.
But God, you amaze us; you don't
only do big things:
flowers are designed,
birds are fed,
your snowflakes and crystals,
molecules and atoms,
are intricate, invisible and strong.
You care for things bigger than we
are,
and things smaller than we are,
and you care for us.
Thank you, most wonderful God.

30

A Fresh Start
After reading Philemon, especially vv 10–16

'At one time he was of no use to you . . .'   Phlmn 11

Father in heaven:
knowing how deeply you love everyone,
we pray to you now for the people who matter to us:
    our families and friends,
    the people we like,
    and the people we admire from a distance
    – especially we pray for *them*,
        because if we only ever see them in the distance,
        on a football or cricket pitch,
        a stage or a screen,
        there's probably not much we can do for them
        except pray;
        and we know that praying is a very strong thing to
            do.

But even more than them, we pray for the people we
    don't like,
the people we've lost patience with,
people who've done us a bad turn,
people we've quarrelled with.

Please help us do
what Paul was asking Philemon to do for Onesimus:
        to have another look at them,
        give them another chance,
        make it up with them
        and begin again
        as friends,

through the grace of Jesus Christ our Lord.

31

Morning
A form for group-led prayers
at a church camp

'. . . long before daylight, Jesus . . . prayed.'   Mk 1:35

Leader: This is a new day.
Group: God gives it.
All: Thank you, Father.

L.   The sun has risen.
G: God made it.
All: Thank you, Father.

L: We are with friends.
G: God's children too.
All: Thank you, Father.

L: Soon there will be breakfast.
G: Another gift from God.
All: Thank you Father.

(INTERLUDE: Brief meditation
and/or orders for the day.)

Group: O Lord our God –
All: please help us –
Leader: by giving good weather today.

G: O Lord our God –
All: please help us –
L: to stay together in a friendship warm enough
          to keep out the cold
          even if it snows.

G: O Lord our God –
All: please help us –
L: to live this day in your company
          and in your way.

G: O Lord our God –
All: please help us –

L: to be sensitive to other people,
    their feelings and their needs,
    to be at one with our human brothers and
        sisters
    throughout the world
    beginning here.

(A MORNING HYMN)

Leader: The grace of Christ be with us.
All, led by Group: Amen.

Offering

a. at Communion

1

Symbols which Speak

'. . . the sign of the promise . . .'   Gen 9:17

These things are for you, heavenly Father.
On the table there is bread and wine,
the appointed picture
of your love in Christ.
On the table also there is money
given by various people in varying amounts,
from earnings, from savings, from pensions,
given with more or less thought
and more or less enthusiasm
but with one common conviction –
that all our getting and giving makes sense
only when it is brought here
into the light of your love in Christ
whose body and blood are pictured
in the bread and wine.

★

We offer to you the bread and the wine and the money
so that they may glorify you
as they speak to us,
and as they speak for us,

about your love
and all that it gives
and all that it demands.

2

Imperfect Gifts

'. . . so how can this Temple that I have built be large enough?'
1 Kgs 8:27

We offer to you the Communion bread and wine.
We offer to you the beauty of this house of prayer.
We offer to you the salute of our presence here,
   and of our attention as we think about your
    Word.
We offer to you our prayers,
   our love,
    our care for one another.
And we offer to you this money.

★

In your great grace, O God, take and use our imperfect
 gifts
to your perfect glory,
through Jesus Christ our Lord.

3

The Sustaining Meal

'He who comes to me will never be hungry . . .' Jn 6:35

Gifts of bread and wine we bring you
so that you may use them for our sustaining
according to your Son's command and promise.
Gifts of money too, we bring,
so that in your hands,

as you lend wisdom to your Church,
they may do your will and receive your blessing
through Jesus Christ.

b. with thanks

4

In Return

'What can I offer the Lord for all his goodness . . .?'   Ps 116:12

For all that makes us thankful,
for all that brings us joy,
for all that gives us hope,
heavenly Father, we return this grateful offering to You.
Use it to make other people happy
in the love of Jesus Christ your Son
who, for the joy that was set before him, died
that we might have life.

5

For Others too

'You have received . . . so give . . .'   Mt 10:8

O God, you fill our lives with wonder and joy.
We try to thank you in words;
here we are trying to thank you with gifts.
Bless what we give,
and use it to help other people also
to experience the sweetness of your love
in Jesus Christ our Lord.

6

Fellowship

'. . . the way in which you have helped me . . .'   Phil 1:5

Our gifts try

This gift tries to speak our thanks
for all we have received from you, our God,
and for all we have received from you
through fellow Christians
and sister churches.
Please use our gift
for the blessing of others as we have been blessed,
through Jesus Christ our Lord.

7

Kindness

'. . . so that they will see the good things you do and praise your
Father . . .'   Mt 5:16

For what you have given we thank you.
From what you have given we give you this,
so that others may come to know your kindness *and your love*
through the kindness of your Church.
Bless our gifts, we pray,
for we offer them in Jesus' name.

8

Purpose

'. . . God works for good with those who love him . . . according to
his purpose.'   Rom 8:28

Lord God:
from all that you have given to us
we offer these gifts for your blessing and use.
May they help to fulfil your purpose

in this church
and in the community
through Jesus Christ.

9

Wisdom

'Who, then, is a faithful and wise servant?'   Mt 24:45

Of all that you have given to us,
this we give back to you, O God.
Grant wisdom to your Church
so that what we give
may glorify you
and help people
to know Jesus Christ.

10

The Token

'They must thank him with sacrifices . . .'   Ps 107:22

For the gifts of your creation,
for the blessings of your grace,
for the gladness of salvation
and the peace of sins forgiven;
for your help to live each day,
for friendship, love and home,
for the Church and what we have
within its fellowship –
for all this, part of our thanks
shall be this gift.
Bless its use, we pray, for Jesus' sake.

11

His Love and Ours

'Every Sunday . . . some money, in proportion to what he has earned
. . . your gift to Jerusalem.'   1 Cor 16:2–3

Life and livelihood are your gifts, O God.
The talents of mind and hand come from You,
and what we reckon to be our attainments
are won with strength and character which you have
    given.

★

These coins and notes which we place before you now
are our recognition
that you are the One we must thank
for everything we rejoice in.
From the wealth you have given us please accept this
    gift.
It speaks *our* love: let it serve *yours*
through Jesus Christ our Lord.

12

Getting and Giving

'Work hard . . . serve the Lord . . . share . . .'   Rom 12:11, 13

Heavenly Father:
these gifts are not merely money.
They show our awareness that you are with us day by
    day
as we earn our living,
enabling us to earn it.
As the hymn says, 'All that we have is thine alone,
                    A trust, O Lord, from Thee'.
Make us wise in getting and giving,
so that we may get without hurt
and give without stint;

and so that getting and giving may be with joy,
               and in peace,
               to your glory,
               through Jesus
               Christ.

c.   of ourselves

13

Fair Exchange

'. . . Offer yourselves as a living sacrifice . . .'   Rom 12:1

O God:
You have given yourself to the world
    in the making and upholding of everything that
    exists.
You have given yourself to the world
    in the redeeming life and death
    of Jesus Christ our Saviour.
You have given yourself to the world
    in the inspiration of poet, prophet and preacher;
    and in the pouring out of your Spirit upon all flesh
      so that all who come to know you in Christ
      may walk in the Spirit
      and realize that they are your children.

★

What can we do in return
but give ourselves to you,
give you what we are and what we have?

★

Accept this which now we offer.
Bless it and use it
for the good of many people,
for Jesus' sake.

14

To One Another

'Teach and instruct one another . . .'   Col 3:16

God:
As we make our offering to you
for the work of your kingdom,
we think also
of what we offer to one another
in fellowship,
and of what we who are older offer to the younger ones
by way of example and teaching.

★

All this offering, to you and to each other,
Accept it, Lord God;
use it to bring light and help
to the world you love,
the world your Son Jesus died to save.

★

In his name we pray.

15

Giving and Keeping

'No one said that any of his belongings was his own . . .'   Acts 4:32

Heavenly Father:
bless what we give,
and make us wise in using what we keep;

so that what we give and what we keep
may be but one offering
as our life is lived in your service
and in your love;
through Jesus Christ our Lord.

16

His Sacrifice, our Gift

'. . . Christ, our Passover lamb, has been sacrificed . . .'   1 Cor 5:7

Lord Jesus Christ:
for love of us
you offered yourself
as the one perfect sacrifice
reconciling us to God.

★

The love you have awakened in our hearts
prompts the gift
which we are offering now.
Accept it, Lord Jesus,
and bless its use
in the life of your Church.

★

By what we have given
and by what we are
may we help other people
to see you.

d. gifts and givers

17

Long-term Benefits

'. . . his love is eternal!'   Ps 107:1

For blessings granted on earth
    and blessings promised in heaven;
for one another
    in the fellowship of your worshipping people;
for all that sustains our life
    and all that sustains our faith
we thank you, O God;
    and in thankfulness we offer these gifts.
    Bless them, bless us,
    for Jesus' sake.

18

Strength and Blessing

'. . . the God of all grace . . . will . . . give you . . . strength . . .'
1 Pet 5:10

With our gifts, O God, we offer ourselves,
so that both gifts and givers
may be used under the guidance of your Spirit
for the strengthening of the Church
and the blessing of mankind,
through Jesus Christ our Lord.

19

Things and People

'I will not offer . . . sacrifices that have cost me nothing.'   2 Sam 24:24

Bless, O Lord, these gifts
and these givers
in the service of your kingdom,
for Jesus Christ's sake.

20

Sharing

'The believers continued . . . in close fellowship and shared their
belongings . . .'   Acts 2:44

O God:
you make us happy
so that we may cheer one another;
you make us strong
so that we may help one another;
and you make us rich enough to give
so that together we may give to your work.
Bless our gifts,
and bless us in the giving of them,
for Jesus' sake.

21

Friends and Helpers

'. . . I call you friends . . .'   Jn 15:15

Thank You, God and Father,
for making us part of your purpose for the world
– using what we are
  and what we give
  and what we do,

treating us as your friends and helpers
in the work of spreading your gospel
to the ends of the earth.
Bless these gifts, we pray, and bless the givers,
in the service of your kingdom,
for Jesus' sake.

e. as action

22

Provision

'. . . to build up the body of Christ.'   Eph 4:12

Lord God, it is no light thing
to offer you a gift.
We bring to your altar a sacrifice
for You to hallow and to use.
Here, from what we have,
are gifts for You to use in this church
and in our sister churches.
Accept what we give, heavenly Father;
bless us in the giving, bless those who use what is
    given.
Strengthen your Church by the gifts of your people
in Jesus Christ.

23

Involvement

'. . . when each separate part works as it should . . .'   Eph 4:16

As serving soldiers, in proud salute to their commander;
as loyal citizens in just tribute to their king;
as grateful neighbours under obligation
    to the good neighbour who befriended them;
as lovers who are glad to make sacrifices
    for a gift to their beloved;
as workers together in the shared support of a great
        cause –
    SO WE WOULD GIVE THESE GIFTS TO YOU, OUR
        GOD,
        in pride, in duty, gratitude and love,
        and with excitement.
Bless what we give,
to the strengthening of your Church militant on earth,
and to the glory of your everlasting name in heaven;
through Jesus Christ our Lord.

24

Activity

'Everything you do or say . . . should be done in the name of the Lord
Jesus . . .'   Col 3:17

O God, we offer you
the worship of our words in prayer,
the worship of our voices in praise,
the worship of our listening minds.
We offer you the worship of beauty in the decoration of
        the church.

★

And we offer you in worship this gift of money,
so that it may be used to strengthen your Church

for the proclamation of your good news
in Jesus Christ.

25

The Bridge

'But they will certainly not be enough . . .' Jn 6:9

O God, at this moment of giving,
two thoughts oppress us:
   – how much must be accomplished
     if our world is to become your kingdom;
   – and how little we have,
     of wealth, strength or virtue
     with which to accomplish anything.

Yet, between the seemingly impossible task
   and our seemingly insignificant strength,
   there stretches like a bridge
   the grace and power of Christ your Son.

Into that yawning gulf
   between your challenge and our impotence,
   or rather, onto the bridge of grace which spans it,
   we pour our gifts, of pocket and of soul.

Your own Spirit supplies the holy and hopeful
     impertinence
   of our giving – a boy's thumb to damn a flood,
            a boy's lunch to feed a multitude.

Accept what we can give, use what we can do,
   to accomplish the impossible things
   which are possible with you,
   through Jesus Christ our Lord.

26

Economics

'. . . she, poor as she is, gave all she had . . .'   Lk 21:4

With 'gold of obedience and incense of lowliness'
we bring to you this 'poor wealth we would reckon as
          ours.'
Use it, O God, and use us,
for the doing of your work in the world you love,
for Jesus Christ's sake.

27

Value Added

'. . . for the sake of what is so much more valuable . . .'   Phil 3:8

Joyfully we give away
to you, our God,
something which in our hands had value
but in your hands shall have glory,
and the honour of heavenly use.
Bless these gifts, and us who give,
for Jesus' sake.

28

Transfiguration

'. . . we saw his glory . . .'   Jn 1:14

As Jesus Christ your Son took human flesh
making it holy and glorious,
so take these imperfect gifts
and transform them
into the holy strength
in which the Church can do your will,
through the same Jesus Christ our Lord.

f. with the family

29

Fullness

'. . . giving us one blessing after another.' Jn 1:16

Thank you, God, for filling things:
　　filling the world with people,
　　filling words with meaning,
　　filling life with happenings,
　　filling our plates with food
　　and our wallets with money.
May we ask one more thing?
　　Please fill our hearts with thankfulness,
　　and, as our gratitude overflows
　　in gifts to you and your Church,
　　bless what we give
　　and make it useful
　　in the doing of what you want done,
　　through Jesus Christ our Lord.

30

How Free is a Gift?
An Offertory Bidding and Prayer

'. . . You know what was paid to set you free . . .'　1 Pet 1:18

Let's think for a moment
about things which have to be paid for,
but which aren't paid for by us.
When we are very young there are a lot of things like
　　that:
food to eat, clothes to wear, a home to live in
– parents do all the paying.

But even when we are grown-up
there are many things we treasure,
but can't pay for (so someone else has to),
or needn't pay for (because someone else already has):
our freedom as citizens, the independence of our
　　nation;
fine traditions,
and the whole inheritance of lovely things
which we call art and civilisation
– these things are ours,
　and they were bought for us by other people,
　with hard work, and sometimes with their lives.
And what about the forgiveness of our sins
　(if we've asked for them to be forgiven)?
What about the right to enter heaven
　(if we've claimed it)?
– THESE THINGS are paid for by JESUS.
　Remember the hymn? – *He died that we might be*
forgiven . . .
That we might go at last to
heaven,
saved by his precious blood.

Now our prayer:　Thank you, God,
　　　　　　　for everything on earth and in heaven
　　　　　　　which we are given free
　　　　　　　because it has been paid for
　　　　　　　by someone else.
　　　　　　　Please accept the gifts we now bring to
　　　　　　　　you
　　　　　　　as part of our thanks,
　　　　　　　in Jesus' name.

31

Stopping to think

'He may bring us sorrow, but his love for us is sure and strong.'
Lam 3:32

Lord God our Father:
when we stop to think about it
we can see
that there is in every day much to delight us,
                              much to excite us,
                              so much to see,
                              so much to do.
Even on difficult days,
when we are ill or bored
or things keep going wrong,
                    even then
                    you send the sunshine
                    or the good sweet rain,
                    and there is usually something for
                              dinner.
So even on a bad day,
there is plenty to be thankful for,
when we stop to think about it.

★

Well, we've stopped to think about it this morning
– about all your goodness to us –
that is why we came to church.
And now we shall say thank you with our gifts.
THANK YOU, GOD,
for all your goodness to us
every day;
thank you
in Jesus' name.

Intercession

a. about the Church

1

Responsive Prayer for Church & Community

'. . . petitions, prayers, requests . . . to God for all people.'   1 Tim 2:1

Father God, we ask you to bless this church:
its members, its leaders, its congregation,
its minister(s),
its friends and its children.
Give it vision, give it growth, give it usefulness.
– O Lord our God/HEAR THE PRAYER OF YOUR
     SERVANTS.

We ask you to give this church joy:
in every department,
from the nursery to the diaconate (elderate etc.),
may there be a non-stop celebration
at which you are Guest of Honour.
– O Lord our God/HEAR THE PRAYER OF YOUR
     SERVANTS.

We ask you to bless the neighbouring churches:
let it be seen that the various denominations
are one Church,
and that we are more deeply united in you
than divided amongst ourselves
– O Lord our God/HEAR THE PRAYER OF YOUR
     SERVANTS.

We pray for the people who hold power,
in our town (district, region) and in the nation:
may they have the strength and wisdom needed
for the job they do,
and may they find fulfilment in the service they give.
– O Lord our God/HEAR THE PRAYER OF YOUR
    SERVANTS.

We pray for the people who are ill, unhappy or lonely,
or in any kind of trouble today.
Please make us quick to see what we can do to help,
and quick to do it.
Bless all who make it their business
to be good neighbours,
and may they discover
how richly friendship is its own reward.
– O Lord our God/HEAR THE PRAYER OF YOUR
    SERVANTS.

2

For one another at Worship

'. . . pray for one another . . .'   Jas 5:16

Here in your house, O God,
we pray for one another.
Give us each one the blessing we need.
We ask your healing for the sick,
        your strength for the tempted
        and your joy for the downcast.
Answer the prayers which we try to put into words,
and the prayers which you read in our hearts,
according to your perfect love
made known in Jesus Christ your Son our Lord.

3

The Healing Fellowship

'. . . Is anyone among you in trouble? . . . prayer made in faith will
heal . . .'   Jas 5:13, 15

Heavenly Father: we pray for one another,
and especially for those amongst us
who have carried to your house
a burden of sorrow or gloom.

★

There are anxieties about health
                    about unemployment,
                    about loved ones.

★

Some of us feel lonely,
even in the company of fellow worshippers,
with perhaps the feeling that nobody cares
or nobody really understands.

★

Bring comfort, O God, by the knowledge of your
        nearness.
Bring comfort by the realisation
that we are never as friendless as we sometimes feel,
nor as hopeless.
Make our fellowship together
and our fellowship with you
a powerful, healing reality
in Jesus Christ.

4

The Priesthood of Believers

'. . . the Lord forbid that I should sin against him by no longer praying
for you.'   1 Sam 12:23

We who have come to worship
represent before you those who have not.
We pray for people who have stayed at home
because they are old or ill.
Give them the sense of being with us in spirit
and keep us faithful to them in prayer and love.

★

As for the people who are not here
because they didn't want to come,
guard us, O God, against thinking we are better than
      they are
– perhaps they didn't need to come
  as badly as we did!
But we acknowledge our responsibility to speak for
      them.
Look upon them in mercy, and give them the blessings
of your love.

★

Look in mercy upon all the turmoil of this peaceless
      world,
and teach us the ways of peace.
Uphold the men and women who bear burdens of
      leadership;
bless the peacemakers, as Jesus promised,
and give them wisdom to calm fear and suspicion
and restrain the aggressiveness
to which fear and suspicion lead.
We pray in Jesus' name.

5

In a Hard Winter

'Pray to God that these things will not happen in the winter!'
Mk 13:18

O God, we commend to your blessing and help
those of this church and its wider fellowship
who have suffered hardship, injury, illness or loss
in these days of wintry weather.
Grant them healing of body and peace of mind,
and the assurance that you do bring good out of
　　　misfortune.

★

We thank you for the good even now being done to the
　　　soil
of gardens, farms and forests
by the snow and frost.
Give, we pray, to people, animals and all growing
　　　things
a spring enriched in due time
by the chills and ills we now deplore;
through Jesus Christ through whom all things were
　　　made
and all things are made new.

6

Prayer by the Church at Worship, for the Junior Church in the schoolrooms

'When your children ask you . . . you will answer . . .'   Ex 12:26–27

To the children and young people
now at work in Junior Church
grant, O God, the gift of curiosity;
and give to their teachers
wisdom, lightness of touch, a sense of humour,

and an infectious enthusiasm
for your truth as it comes to us
in Jesus Christ.

7

Church and Denomination

'. . . the pressure of my concern for all the churches.'   2 Cor 11:28

O God:
we pray for your Church in every place.
Make her able to bear persecution;
and in places where the going seems easy and the way
        safe,
keep her alert and active.

★

Bless and guide our own denomination:
its administrators, committees, missionaries and
        ministers.
Make it a strong servant and a faithful messenger
in the service of your gospel and your kingdom
as they are made known
in Jesus Christ.

8

On a Missionary Deputation Sunday

'Go, then, to all peoples everywhere and make them my
        disciples . . .'   Mt 28:19

O God:
we pray for all whose business it is today
to open eyes and imaginations
to the work of your Church throughout the world.
We pray for the missionary deputation visiting this
        district
and for your servant who will speak to us.

★

Give them the joy
of seeing their facts and their visions
received with attention.
Challenge, enlighten and encourage congregations
by their words,
through the power of your living Word to mankind
– Jesus Christ our Lord.

9

A Discontented Prayer

'. . . I do not praise you . . .'   1 Cor 11:17

Forgive us, Lord God our Father,
that your holy Church throughout all the world
proclaims you so unconvincingly
and serves you so half-heartedly.

★

Bless richly the people, the congregations and the
     orders
that shame the rest of us
by the way they live out the life of Christ
and demonstrate the power the Holy Spirit gives.

★

Pour out the Holy Spirit
to make the rest of your Church
like the best of your Church
– something able to turn the world
   upside down,
    something fit to be called
    the Body of Christ.
                 We ask it for his sake.

b. about people

10

Leadership

'. . . the men who are considered rulers . . .'   Mk 10:42

Almighty God:
we pray for those called to leadership in your human
     family,
the nations of the world;
and for those called to leadership
in your all too human family, the Church.
Whatever their power,
may their graciousness in using it
help to make your grace credible;
through Jesus Christ our Lord.

11

Revolution and Authority

'If one of you wants to be great . . .'   Mt 20:26

Hear our prayer, O God and Father of all,
for men and women called to leadership.
We think of some, leaders for a time,
who have had the power they used to hold taken from
     them,
and who must make new terms
with a life in which others govern.
We think of some, revolutionaries yesterday,
newly come to power and faced with the problem
of how to turn revolution into government.

★

We pray for the leaders of the nations
in their immense responsibility
as makers and keepers of peace,
and we ask you to overrule the schemes of those
who do not even want peace.

★

We remember those called to leadership in the Church,
and especially the deacons (elders, churchwardens etc.)
chosen by this congregation.
Humble and comfort them
by the knowledge that all power comes from you
and that none could have authority
except it were given them from above.

★

Strengthen and confirm all who, in their exercise of
          power,
try to place themselves and others under your law,
and who seek first your kingdom and its righteousness;
through Jesus Christ our Lord.

12

Youth movements and leaders

'Never forget these commands. . . . Teach them to your
children.'   Deut 6:6–7

Father God:
we commend to your blessing and help
the leaders and members of the **Guide movement
in this country and throughout the world.
For the leaders of **Guiding
and all their colleagues in the service of youth
we ask
vision, energy, patience and stamina.

(** for adaptation as appropriate to other organisations)

Grant also that they may be encouraged in their work
by those flashes of reward
which can brighten our labours:
the discovery of special talent,
the emergence of initiative
and, from a child unusual or ordinary,
the sudden, unexpected word or gesture of appreciation
which shows that care does not go unnoticed
even by the very young.
Grant above all
the reward of seeing the generations rise
clear-eyed and with courageous heart
to meet the world's tomorrow
in the strength and Spirit of Jesus Christ,
in whose name we pray.

13

Communication
After reading Acts 17:16–34

'Some of the things we hear you say sound strange . . .'   Acts 17:20

O God: your servant Paul preached to the men of
    Athens.
A Jew had to find words which would convince Greeks.
We pray for all who try to communicate with strangers:
    the old with the young,
    the southerner with the northerner,
    employee with employer,
    black with white:
wherever speech is impeded
by privilege or deprivation,
complacency or resentment.

★

May there be that gift of tongues,
as much love as linguistics,

whereby sophisticated people may perceive simple
        truths,
or the mind of a child encompass the wisdom of angels.

★

Give us, each one, the wit and the will
at the right moment to tell the truth we grasp
and speak of the Lord we love
to people we know
and strangers we meet;
for your glory's sake.

14

The Holy Spirit and Human Need

'The Helper will come – the Spirit . . .' Jn 15:26

Holy Spirit:
you make the powerful presence of Jesus Christ real
and perceptible
in a world which still needs him
and which he still loves.
To you we pray for those amongst us who are anxious
        or sad.
We pray also for those who are ill in mind or body,
for those about to enter hospital or there already,
especially if they are very young.

★

We pray for those called
to the ministry of nursing, doctoring
and hospital administration,
and for those who, without special training,
bear heavy burdens at home looking after the ill and
        elderly.
We remember some who have to manage somehow on
        their own;
and ask your blessing

for all the ordinary folk who are good neighbours
and friends in need.

★

In the bearing and the alleviating of human pain
may the Father's will be done,
may the Father's love be known,
and may his grace be mighty to help;
through Jesus Christ his Son our Lord.

15

Human Need and Human Love

'You yourselves give them something . . .'   Mt 14:16

Hear our prayer, O God,
for all who are ill, and all whose vocation is healing;
for those in trouble, and those whose business is
        helping.
Raise us all up to the high calling
of being good neighbours,
in the name and the Spirit of Jesus Christ your Son.

16

Victims of Prejudice

'Moses had married a Cushite woman. . . .'   Num 12:1

Almighty Father:
the scripture tells how unhappiness came
to your servant Moses,
when his family disapproved
of his marriage to a foreigner.

Look in mercy, we pray,
on all who suffer because of other people's prejudices.
Bring in your justice

wherever people of one race
despise and hurt those of another.

Open the eyes
of all who govern nations
where there is tension between race and race,
creed and creed.
Unite the peoples of South Africa,
of the new African states, and of Ireland,
on new foundations of mutual tolerance and respect.

Give wisdom and good humour
to communities within our own nation
whose peace is threatened
by the irritation of indifference
or the pain of inequality;

through him in whom all are made one,
Jesus Christ our Saviour.

17

Those who Suffer
After reading Judges 16:4–21

'The Philistines captured him and put his eyes out. They took him to
Gaza . . .'   Judg 16:21

Almighty God:
we watch with reverence and respect, and not without
     fear,
the way you deal with men and women
on whom your favour rests.
For although those you love do not always die young,
they do not have an easy life.

★

Your servant Abraham had to wait, faith flagging,
long time,
for the keeping of your promise to him.

Your servant Moses,
liberator and leader of your people Israel,
endured that people's carping criticism
and rampant rebellion,
and died seeing fulfilment only in the distance.
Your servant David was outlawed,
your servant Elijah nearly gave in to despair,
and your Son our Saviour cried out from a cross
where it seemed you had forsaken him.

★

Of all your servants
Samson was not the only one
to be left alone in the dark.

★

Yet from such loneliness and forsaking
you have brought your saints victorious;
in such loneliness and forsaking
you have won your victories with them.
The resurrection you intend
bursts forth from the death you permit.

★

Dear Father:
we ask you to uphold in this faith
all those who today are passing through dark shadows
of sorrow, despair or torment.
Give to them the spirit that sings your praise
in a dungeon,
and calls down blessings
on those who persecute and slay.
Set free those who suffer,
and give meanwhile the assurance deep in the heart
that suffering is not waste,
and that your purposes do not fail
– nor your love
                    in Jesus Christ our Lord.

18

At the End of their Tether

'From the depths of my despair I call to you, Lord.'   Ps 130:1

Lord God:
hear us as our hearts go out in sympathy
to the homeless who have little prospect of being
        housed,
to men and women unemployed
and with no hope of finding a job,
to travellers out of fuel on lonely roads,
to businessmen who have lost incentive,
and all who are near to despair
at the state of the world, or the nation, or themselves.
★

Show us in our desperation how to pray,
how to imagine and how to act,
so that coming to the end of our tether
may bring us to the beginning of your hope
in Jesus Christ.

19

People of Importance

'Jesus asked, "Whose face and name are these?"'   Mk 12:16

Lord Jesus: you are King
of a kingdom which you set up by coming to earth
in the form of a servant.

We bring before you in our prayer
all who seek and gain high office
democratically, or by conspiracy, or even by violence;
and all who hold power over us,
whether we approve of them or not.
We pray also for those who frighten us
because the power they hold makes no sense,
being based on terror, or on fashion.

Remembering that those we hate are still loved by you,
we pray not only for the people who mourn
loved ones killed by terrorists,
but also for the killers.
We commend to your mercy every evil ruler and
 government,
asking that their downfall may involve a minimum of
 fighting,
and may give them a chance to repent.

Guard and guide our politicians
amid the pressures and tensions of their work.
Rid their debates of thoughtless prejudice
and needless offence.
Enable them to strive not so much *against* one another
as *for* truth, and for the righteousness
which exalts a nation.

To you who taught that all rule should be service,
and all personal importance a reason for humility, not
 pride,
we pray in your own gracious name.

20

Artists

'Workmen with every kind of skill . . .'   1 Chr 28:21

Father of all goodness:
we thank you that there is beauty in the world,
and that you have given us eyes, ears and imaginations
to recognise it.

We thank You for art and artists,
working to help us to see better,
                      hear better,
                      and understand better
                      the harmonies and rhythms
                      of shape and colour,
                      sound and speech,

which can express our thoughts
and sometimes reflect yours.

We pray for musicians – composers and interpreters,
for painters and sculptors,
the writers of books and poems,
the makers of plays and films,
all actors, singers and dancers.
May they have joy in what they do.

Guard them against the artists' temptations:
the turning of the mind from truth and its cost
to popularity and its reward;
the mistaking of a modest talent
for something greater,
and the loss of a simple gift
in complicated pretensions.

We pray for all whose heightened sensitivity
to what is lovely
makes them more vulnerable than others
by pain, disillusion, bitterness and despair.

Grant to them,
and to us all,
the ability to rest in you
and in the vision of your glory;
so that we may none of us fall into the folly
of seeking glory for ourselves,
or of taking ourselves more seriously than we
should.
Set us free from mankind's first silly sin
of wishing to be gods and goddesses.

Give us all the happy knack
of being happy people,
with time and room in our lives
to offer sacrifice and share love
– yet always held safe
in your greater love
and your entirely sufficient sacrifice
in Jesus Christ our Brother Man and Saviour God.

c. about problems

21

Nation and People

'You have authority . . . only because it was given to you . . .'
Jn 19:11

Lord of lords and King of kings:
your word teaches us as a solemn duty
to pray for those set in authority.
So we pray for our Queen and her Parliament,
that in difficult times those bearing heavy responsibility
may be given strength and wisdom
to match their tasks.
We pray also for those whose power is real but
        unofficial
and therefore dangerous in ways hard to control.
We pray for those who seem ignorant and stupid
but who suddenly find power in their hands,
and for those who become frustrated
in their dealings with such people,
and are tempted to hasty action.
Help us to find ways to hold in balance
the good order of established procedures,
and those forces and opinions
which established procedures repress
but which have a right to be represented.

★

Grant, O God, to all who hold power,
however they obtained it and whatever sort it is,
an extraordinary access of good sense.
We need miracles of mildness;
and in the hour of our nation's need we turn to you,
who poured out your mighty Spirit

in the likeness of a gentle dove,
and sent your Son to be our Prince of peace.
In his name we pray.

22

During Industrial Strife

'They took their money and started grumbling against the
employer.'   Mt 20:11

God of all compassion, plenteous in mercy:
we ask your help for all who suffer
in body, mind or circumstance
because of our present troubles.
Bless them with good neighbours, good humour and
       patience.
Quicken our own imagination, and our wits,
to see what we can do
whether to help individuals
or to sweeten the mood of our whole community.
Grant to us who suffer and to those who must negotiate
a sincere understanding of those to whom we are
     opposed,
whichever side we are on.
Give us grace to let the faith we hold
affect the way we react to what annoys us;
to the glory of your name
and for the sake of Jesus Christ our Saviour.

23

In a time of National Disunity

'If a country divides itself into groups which fight each other, that
country will fall apart.'   Mk 3:24

Give to us all, O God,
wherever we stand in our present disagreements,

a clear vision of the things we believe to be right
and great patience with the people we believe to be
       wrong.

★

As swiftly as may be,
restore us to a common mind,
but not to a common mind imposed by violence
nor one which is merely an agreement to ignore
what really divides us.

★

Just as a man sees better for having two eyes,
so may these two strong opinions
make our unity, when it is restored,
a wiser one.

★

Use your Church in these days, and make her fit to be
       used:
may her counsel be far-seeing,
       her judgments temperate,
       and her way with people gentle;
as befits the gospel she proclaims
in Christ's name.

24

Before a General Election

'Happy is the nation whose God is the Lord.'   Ps 33:12

Lord of the nations and heavenly Father of all mankind:
we pray for our nation and its peoples.
Have in your hand our electioneering and the election.
Enable us to make honest choices;
use the choices we make and the men and women we
       choose

for the doing of your will in our land.
We ask that in the next government
there may be the vision of a united Britain
waging no class war
and waging no race war.
We ask for men and women to lead us
whose words and example may encourage hard work
and fair play.

Restore to our community a wish
to build, collaborate and give;
set us free from meanness, greed and cynicism.
Restore, where we have lost it,
our common respect of the law,
not by its more rigorous enforcement,
but through a wholesome concern amongst us
for the general good.
Grant a spirit of neighbourliness, optimism and
      enterprise.
Teach us to love one another and appreciate one
      another,
in all our diversity and despite all our differences.
Make us once more a nation which is blessed
because its God is the Lord.
We ask it in the name of Jesus Christ your Son.

25

Conflict and Suffering, Prayer and Action

'If you will only obey me . . .'   Is 1:19

O God of life and love:
while our conflicts remain unresolved
men and women are killed, the innocent suffer,
and children go in fear.
Therefore awaken the imagination
of those amongst us who are violent,
and stir the conscience

of those amongst us who are complacent.
Open our eyes to the wrong we do
by leaving things as they are
   in Ireland,
   in the Middle East,
   and on all the frontiers
      of geography,
      of tension
      and of injustice,
      between East and West,
      North and South.
Be with those who grieve,
who suffer, and who are afraid.
Inspire and strengthen every agency of help, healing
   and reconciliation.

★

We pray also for those whose sufferings derive
not from dramatic doings between nations and
     ideologies,
but from the hazards of accident, disease, handicap and
     age.

★

Grant patience and resilience to the unfortunate;
give skill and compassion to all who try to help.

★

And to each one of us give the right word to say,
and the wit to see the right thing to do,
for those in sorrow, difficulty or need.
So may your children pray
and also act for the fulfilment of their prayers.
We ask this in the name of him who spent long hours
in prayer to you,
but also went about doing good:
Jesus Christ our Lord.

26

World Tensions

'Am I supposed to take care of my brother?'   Gen 4:9

Father: we bring to you in our prayer
the places and problems
which to our worried minds are just names
read in the newspaper or meticulously pronounced
by television commentators
– but which in your sight mean people,
people whom you love.
We remember the time-embittered tensions in Ireland,
and the perilous stresses in Africa.

★

We know that the world is divided
between the overfed and the hungry,
between those who make money out of armaments
and those who dread violence.

In the mystery of your grace
bring sanity and the love of peace to your beloved,
foolish world.
Guide our rulers and representatives
and make them wise, patient and just.

★

Transform the world, we pray,
and begin with us.
Even if all we have to defend
is the vegetable garden against the children next door;
even if all we have to share
is a cup of tea and a biscuit when the pension runs to it;
make your praying people
the model for a loving world.

Through Jesus Christ our Lord.

27

War and Peace

'. . . the noise of battles close by and news of battles far away.'
Mk 13:7

We pray, O God, for our human brothers and sisters
in parts of the world
where the harshness of nature and the strife of nations
have brought sufferings longer and deeper
than we have yet known.
We pray for the peoples of Ireland and Palestine,
of south and central Africa, South America and Asia,
and especially those multitudes among them
who are oppressed, in want, or forced to flee their
      homes.

★

Give to the world you love a spirit of reason and
      patience.
Restrain and convert the parties and the men
who seek their own advantage
in the shaking of other people's peace.

★

But also open the eyes of nations so seemingly secure
and used to thinking of themselves as right,
that they do not see the deprivations and injustices
which they have imposed on others.

★

Strengthen the United Nations
and all the agencies of peace and human help.
Continue to hold in your merciful love
the wayward and needy heart of mankind.
For Jesus' sake.

28

Human Dignity

'. . . Mortal man, stand up.'   Ezek 2:1

Heavenly Father:
we pray for all those whom the world has worked upon
to convince them that they are not much good:
  slaves and second-class citizens in whatever nation,
  people who have always been led to suppose
    they were the dull member of the family
    or invariably bottom of the class,
  men and women who have been brought to see
    themselves
    as failures professionally, socially, or morally.

★

O God, you are the King of heaven:
you have called all who will listen into your royal
    household,
and given them royal status.
And your call is something from which no-one is
    disqualified:
Jesus Himself sought out the despised and rejected,
the socially disgraced, and those of little account
in the world's eyes.
Please help your Church to raise people
in their own estimation
by declaring the value
which your love has set upon us all
through Jesus Christ our Lord.

29

Bewildered People

'. . . his heart was filled with pity for them, because they were like
sheep without a shepherd.'   Mk 6:34

Almighty God: you create the solid mountains
and the tempests which shake them;
your power keeps still what is still
and moves whatever is moved.
We claim your strong help for all timid and unsettled
    folk.
We cry out for the children
caught up in the quarrels and wars of their elders;
for old people bewildered in changing cities;
and for young people who cannot see where life leads
    to.
We pray for the sick in body and the feeble in mind,
and for all who are oppressed
by persecution, injustice, discrimination or ill luck.
    Grant to all who lack it today
    the sense that life is underpinned by your power,
    guided by your purpose,
    and surrounded by your love
    which is revealed
    in Jesus Christ.

30

Frightened People

'Do not be afraid, little flock . . .'   Lk 12:32

Father: grant your peace
to all the people who look out at the world
and are frightened.
They see change and violence all around,
the flouting of your laws
and the forgetfulness

of neighbour
and kindred.
Strengthen in their hearts
    the conviction that you are God,
        that you have everything
        in your hands,
        whether it looks like that
        or not.
Help them to believe and see
that even in the darkest days your kingdom advances,
and that your purposes of love and peace for all
    mankind
are well within your power to accomplish
through Jesus Christ our Lord.

31

Illusions and Aspirations

'. . . those who are last will be first, and those who are first will be
last.'   Mt 20:16

Lord God, King of all who rule
and champion of all who are oppressed:
give a sense of proportion
to all those who are screened from reality
by the illusions of great power or great wealth.

Enable those whose position seems high and important
and those whose position seems lowly and insignificant
to realise and relish their common humanity.

Prosper all efforts that are made
to give regional, racial and social groups
a just measure of freedom and self-determination.

Grant patience and wisdom to all who govern and lead
Basques, Bengalis and Palestinians,
Irish, Scots, Welsh, English
and Nonconformists.

And to all of us who reckon ourselves in a minority,
grant grace to match our pride
– for while we can feel that we are oppressed,
    it takes others to see
    that we are proud.

Guide us as we move,
on the one hand toward European unity
and on the other toward devolution and regionalism
within each nation.

Restrain extreme opinion from extreme violence,
and let not enthusiasm drive out humour
from politics, religion or anything else.

We ask it in the name of Christ your Son
who declared judgment with love
and truth with wit.

Commitment & Petition

a. as worship begins

1

Opening the Conversation

'. . . God exists and rewards those who seek him.'   Heb 11:6

O GOD WE THANK YOU
    that of all our striving
    you are the true goal;
    that to all our questioning
    you are the real answer;
    that you are the source and giver of our life,
    its only Redeemer and its rightful King.

O GOD WE TRUST YOU
    to make our jangled life
    into harmony and melody,
    and to weave the tangled skein of human history
    into an eternal pattern full of sense and glory.

O GOD WE CONFESS
    that our life is sinful
    and our mind divided.
    We are not like angels

whose only joy is to obey your command.
We are in turmoil amongst ourselves
and within ourselves.

WE ARE AMAZED
that your purpose includes us
and that your love saves us.

AND YET WE KNOW
that you loved the world enough
to send your only Son,
who held out the hand of your friendship
and paid the ghastly price of our redemption.

O GOD TOUCH US NOW
with your Holy Spirit
to open our hearts once more to your cleansing,
to open our minds once more to your word.
Speak in judgment on our sin;
speak in peace to the penitent.

O GOD RAISE UP
our fallen humanity;
set us on our feet to walk in your way,
                    to leap with your joy,
                    and to praise you
                        in your house
                        and in our life,

through Jesus Christ our Lord.

2

The Enormity of it

'. . . complete freedom to go into the Most Holy Place . . .'   Heb 10:19

Lord God:
when we are used to churchgoing
the idea of praising you seems reasonable enough.
Almost without thinking we kneel

– in our hearts if not with our knees –
to praise you. To PRAISE YOU!

God:
it is preposterous. How dare we?
Praise you as we praise one another?
Politely congratulate you
on creating the heavens and the earth?
Applaud your human performance
in the person of Jesus your Son?
Gratefully acknowledge your kind invitation to
          paradise?

How can we praise you?
We cannot praise you in words we would use
to one another;
yet these are the only words we have.
We must praise you because it is our duty and your due,
yet the only words we have
are an impertinence.

But then, in our embarrassed silence,
we remember
the faith of millions now
and the example of the saints before us
daring with confidence, with just such impertinence,
to approach you, sure of their welcome.

And we remember
that it was your own Son who said,
'Come to the Father through me, for I am the Way'.

And we remember
that it is your own Spirit who works within us
to convince us that we are your children
and that you love us.

So we dare,
so we can,
so we do
come into the secret and holy place
stammering out our praise

and thankfulness,
rejoicing to know that you are in control
of the vast universe
and of this little world;
rejoicing to know that you do not despise the speech
even of wayward children
in whom there is so much
for you to pardon.

Father:
help us to worship You,
for Jesus' sake.

b. after readings

3

Daniel 5

'. . . the king saw the hand as it was writing. He turned
pale . . .'   Dan 5:5–6

O God, you know everything about us,
and you know how we love to see
a man like king Belshazzar
get his desserts.
He had it coming to him, we say,
going on his own proud way ignoring you.
But, holy God,
what have *we* got coming to *us*,
the proud way *we* go on, ignoring you?

★

Have mercy, gracious God, upon the world and us;
forgive our sins and teach us,
while yet there is time,
to walk in your way
and turn to your light
as it shines
in Jesus Christ our Saviour.

4

Matthew 16:13–20, Mark 8:27–30

'Peter answered, "You are the Messiah".'   Mk 8:29

Jesus Christ, Son of the living God:
Set our tongues wagging
    with the truth of your gospel,
    the hallelujahs of your resurrection
    and the joy of being saved.
But silence our questioning chatter
    which prevents our hearing you
    and delays our obedience.

When the time for talking is done
and only decision will do,
    enable us to heed you,
    to say yes to you,
    and live out in strong and loving deeds
    the faith we profess.

5

Matthew 18:12–14, Luke 15

'When he finds it, he is so happy . . .'   Lk 15:5

O God, we thank you for your word of hope:
that coins and sheep are found as well as lost,
that prodigals return to a welcome,

that there is joy in heaven
    over one sinner who repents,
and that years which the locust has eaten
    can be restored.
We thank you for the word of hope
made actual and accessible to us
in Jesus Christ your Son.
Give grace that we may lay hold of the Good News
and BE FOUND
in him.

6

Luke 11:37–53, Luke 12:1–3

'Be on guard against . . . hypocrisy.'   Lk 12:1

It is not only the Pharisees, Lord Jesus.
We too like our little pretences.
We cannot stand very much reality so we prefer to
    play –
  play at living,
  play at loving,
  play at serving,
  play at worshipping.
Once more forgive us, Lord,
and by your promised Holy Spirit
fill our hearts and minds
  with a real faith
  that can make a real difference
  in the real world.
Make us fit
  for a real eternity
  in the real heaven;
for your name and glory's sake.

7

John 4

'. . . the true worship that he wants.'   Jn 4:23

Lord Jesus Christ:
the day has come which you promised was coming,
when it is not the place of prayer that matters
– mountain, temple, holy grove –
not the place of prayer
but the heart of him who prays:
'neither in this mountain nor in Jerusalem
but in Spirit and in truth'.

★

Which does not make it easier to pray,
for there cannot be comfort now in knowing
that the words are right,
or the priest properly paid,
the sacrifice duly offered.
Our coming can only be with open heart:
open with our sin, open to your love.
'O God, make clean our hearts within us . . .
and grant us thy salvation'.

★

No secrets from you,
no pride before you;
but the simple acceptance of what you offer –
    the love of a Father who waits to forgive,
    and to clothe us in the best robe
    of his own Son's righteousness.

★

For such worship equip us with your Spirit,
as you have equipped us with your words
which now we pray in your name,
saying:

    OUR FATHER. . . .

8

John 14 and 15

'Believe in God and believe also in me.'   Jn 14:1

Lord Jesus Christ:
we believe in you
and in the heavenly Father who sends you.
We believe that you and he are one
with the Holy Spirit
who makes you known to us.
We love and praise in you
the highest and the best beyond all knowing.
In loving you
we set our hearts
on that which will not change
nor diminish
nor turn against us.
Our hearts should not be troubled then, O Lord;
but they easily are.

★

Forgive and increase our little faith,
replenish our supply of grace,
give us your peace.
Graft our lives into your life
so that as branches of the one true Vine
we may bear much fruit
in the Spirit
to the Father's glory.

★

Now as we take your own words and speak them in
        prayer,
grant us more than your words to speak with:
may we live with your life,
may we act with your power,
may we love with your love,

growing more and more like you
who first could truly say:

OUR FATHER. . . .

9

John 21:15–25

'Lord, you know everything; you know that I love you!'   Jn 21:17

Dear God,
almighty yet so gentle with your children:
we think we understand Peter's uneasiness
when in the words of Jesus you challenged his love
                            and claimed his service.
You know that we love you, for you know everything,
but that means that you know also
                    the imperfection of our love,
                    the bankruptcy of our virtue,
                    the smallness of our strength.
In your mercy you credit us with love,
                    you treat us as apostles and tell us
                    to feed your sheep,
                    tend your lambs,
                    shine as lights in the world
                    and remain faithful until death.
You treat your Church
as though she were capable of being your Church
– and we are terrified,
  or we would be
  except that in Jesus you have also said:
                    'My strength shall be perfected
                    in your weakness. . . .
                    My grace is sufficient'.

★

Lord, teach your Church
– teach us –

our powerlessness
so that we may learn to depend entirely on your power.
Teach us
our sinfulness
so that, forgiven, we may show forth a holiness
that is entirely yours.
So may our light shine before men
that they may see our deeds
but glorify you;
through Jesus Christ our Lord.

10

Romans 12:1–2, 1 Corinthians 15:35–50

'. . . let God transform you . . .'   Rom 12:2

Lord Jesus:
we look at ourselves
and at one another,
and we see our need to be transformed
by the renewing of our mind.
We read the scripture's promise
that we who were born in the likeness of Adam
and are born again through faith, by grace,
shall show also the likeness
of the second Adam,
the proper Man,
your blessed Self.
Saviour, lifted up in the death which gives life,
draw us to yourself;
      make us able to desire,
              able to *bear* being drawn –
              since nearer to you is nearer to your cross.
Reinforce our little faith and love
so that we may fully desire to be fully remade
in your likeness.
Then, as a potter with clay,

make of us what you will,
make of us what only you can,
for the glory of the Father's name.

11

Ephesians 3

'. . . I pray that Christ will make his home in your hearts . . .'
Eph 3:17

Heavenly Father:
we can scarcely understand what we ask
when we ask that the Spirit of your Son may dwell in us,
that we may have the mind of Christ,
that Christ may dwell in our hearts by faith.
We do not know what it may mean
or where it may lead:
to our share of the cross, perhaps.

★

Yet this is what you teach us to ask,
and your word in scripture promises
that Christ in us
is our hope of glory.

★

Then, of your mercy, let it be so.
Even so come, Lord Jesus.

12

2 Timothy 3:10–4:5

'All Scripture is . . . useful . . .'   2 Tim 3:16

Lord, we thank you for your word in scripture,
the record and the distillation
of man's experience, vision, failure and faith

through countless generations.
We thank you for what the Bible says to us
of warning, encouragement and hope.
We thank you that it was not all written by saints
and was none of it written for angels.
We thank you for calling us through scripture
to the practice of a religion for ordinary people
in the real circumstances
of human life,
where your greatest victories have been won
by Jesus Christ your Son,
our Saviour.

c. after hymns

13

'GREAT IS THY FAITHFULNESS'
To the God who builds, and keeps, and is faithful

'If the Lord does not build the house, the work of the builders is
useless.'   Ps 127:1

O GOD, WE GIVE YOU GLORY because of your
    mighty power.
They that wait upon you shall renew their strength
because *your* strength is so great,
and because,
    as a strong king uses his power for his people,
    and as a strong father uses his power for his children,
    so you in your might are devoted in love
    to the sons and daughters of men
    whom you have made.

IN YOUR MIGHTY POWER YOU CREATED ALL
THAT IS,
from the inconceivably vast to the unimaginably small,
from rocks whose lifetime is measured in millions of
        years
to particles of matter and particles of life
which last for minutes or seconds or fractions of a
        second.
    In your hand
    are the building and decay of nations,
    the breeding and dispersal of races;
    kings and rulers are called to greatness
    and banished to obscurity
    in the pattern of your purpose.

SO IF PEOPLE ARE TO KNOW SAFETY,
OR GOVERNMENTS ARE TO RETAIN CONTROL,
IF TRADITION IS TO BE MAINTAINED,
OR OUR CIVILISATION IS TO LAST,
it is your keeping that they must look to.
    Have in your hand, Almighty God,
    the people and the things we treasure.
    Bring under your judgment
    our treasuring of them –
    for in treasuring them we may be wise or foolish.
    Does the fondness of our love
    harm the people who are dear to us?
    Does the way of life we cherish
    rest too heavily on men and women suffering
    under injustice we did not know we had inflicted
    because it was too far away,
    or too familiar, for us to notice?
    Have you a better thing for the world
    than what we cling to?
    May your will be done
    and your kingdom come
    in spite of us, if what we want is wrong.

DAY BY DAY WE REST IN YOUR FAITHFULNESS
WHICH WILL OUTLAST the universe

and time
and our little life on earth.
Our hope in you is an eternal hope,
and the life for which in Christ we trust you
is eternal life.
So give us each day our daily bread,
and the shelter and health which You know we need;
but give us grace not to set our heart on these things,
nor limit our vision to the things of here and now,
of sight and touch.

Help us
to live and work as your children
in this passing world;
then raise us to live and give you glory
in eternity with the saints and angels;

through Jesus Christ our Lord.

14

'BLESSED ASSURANCE, JESUS IS MINE'
or 'GOD IS MY STRONG SALVATION'

'. . . not with words only, but also with power and the Holy Spirit,
and with complete conviction . . .'   1 Thes 1:5

GOD AND FATHER:
we greatly need you.
We need reassuring
that we are loved,
that we are understood and forgiven.
We need reassuring
that in the dangerous business of being alive
safety is possible,
and that even when we cannot be safe
we can be saved,
and that death itself is not the end of life.
We need reassuring
that the things which frighten us most

are really part of your loving plan
– things like the size of the universe;
the brief frailty,
not only of individual people
but of whole civilisations;
the swift passage of time
and the certainty
that all things temporal
are also temporary.
We need reassuring
that the things of time are temporary because
you have something far more wonderful in
store
for eternity.
SUCH ASSURANCE WE NEED
and we seek it from you.
In part – in marvellous part –
you give us the assurance we
need.
Your love, your mercy and your
peace
come to us in Jesus Christ.
Apostle, preacher and prophet
tell us
that we who believe in Jesus
have our citizenship in heaven,
that we have begun to live eternal
life,
and that none can pluck us from
your hand.
BUT THE ASSURANCE, THOUGH BLESSED, IS
STILL ONLY PARTIAL:
it is a promise not yet fulfilled, so that we must hope;
it is a certainty not yet to be seen by mortal eyes,
nor touched yet by human hands,
so that we must have faith.
Therefore, heavenly Father
WE SEEK FROM YOU NOT ONE ASSURANCE
BUT TWO

– the great and deep and long assurance
   that, by your grace, we are saved through faith
   and heading for heaven;
– and also, meanwhile, the assurance of grace
   to walk patiently in faith and hope and love, day by
      day,
   with simple obedience
   and small gifts made holy
   by being offered back to you and accepted.
SO GIVE US, God and Father,
               the faith to face eternity
               and the grace to meet each day,
               through the same Jesus Christ our
                  Saviour
               in whose name we ask it.

15

'GOD IS GOOD; WE COME BEFORE HIM'

'Let us come near . . . We can trust God . . .'   Heb 10:22–23

O God our Father:
of your goodness, pity us in our sin
and forgive us, for Jesus' sake;
renew in us the peace of knowing that we are pardoned;
make us better able to live in your righteousness
and behave to one another as those whom You love.

O God our King:
in your greatness protect and rule our lives;
hear our prayers, spoken and unspoken,
for the things which concern us and the people we love;
prompt and guide us in work which shall serve your
      kingdom
and prosper your purpose.

O God all-wise:
give us ears to hear your word,
a mind to understand and the will to obey it;

so that your truth may set us free
to live as your children,
serve as your subjects,
and pray with your saints,
now and for ever;
through Jesus Christ our Lord.

16

'DEAR MASTER, IN WHOSE LIFE I SEE
ALL THAT I LONG, BUT FAIL, TO BE'

'When anyone is joined to Christ, he is a new being . . .'   2 Cor 5:17

Saviour:
we thank you for showing us
in the perfection of your life
that by ourselves we can do nothing good or holy;
and since apart from you we can do nothing,
we praise and thank you for the promise
that in your love and power
we can do all things.
Take our sin away,
raise us with you to newness of life;
so that our lives,
taking all their goodness from You,
may give you all the glory
for ever and ever.

17

'THY KINGDOM COME, O GOD
THY RULE, O CHRIST, BEGIN'

'. . . be concerned above everything else with the Kingdom of God
and with what he requires of you . . .'   Mt 6:33

As we have sung, so we would pray
for your kingdom to come, O God,

your reign of peace and purity and love;
but we know the prayer is empty
unless we are offering ourselves
to be your subjects.
Your kingdom means that *we* seek peace,
that *we* keep pure,
that *we* cease from hatred;
it means *our* deeds of shame forsaken,
and *our* cold love fired
to a sacrificial burning.

★

Lord Christ of cross and resurrection,
to pray for your Father's kingdom to come
is a fearful thing.
Yet what else can we pray for
if what we really want
is heaven on earth
and heaven in heaven for ever?
What else can we pray for
if what we really want
is an end to all fear save the holy fear of God?
What else is there to pray for
if, even only in rare bright moments,
we dream of a saved world?

★

Lord, your kingdom bring triumphant,
and let it triumph over us.
Let our lust, oppression and crime
flee from before your face.
Your kingdom come, O God,
your rule, O Christ, begin.
Make us able to bear your rule;
cultivate in us the noble character
which befits your subjects –
conscience clear, mind serene,
heart free to love and serve,
and filled with the hilarity of heaven.

★

Gather us into the centre of your purpose.
Set our desires on your Father's kingly rule
and the righteousness which it demands and makes
     possible;
to our eternal blessing
and the glory of your name –
the name in which your Spirit moves us to pray.

18

'O JESUS, KING MOST WONDERFUL'

'You will eat and drink at my table in my Kingdom . . .'   Lk 22:30

O Jesus, King most wonderful:
teach us to value your kingdom as if it were a treasure
which we had discovered –
and no-one else knew where it was.

O Jesus, King most wonderful:
teach us what we must give up for your kingdom,
as if we were the merchant who was willing to sell all he
     had
in order to purchase the priceless pearl.

O Jesus, King most wonderful:
teach us how to speak of your kingly rule
– of all it means to us,
and of all it enables us to believe in;
so that we may persuade other people to call you King.

O Jesus, King most wonderful:
teach us to prize and study the truth about God you
     have told
– to dwell in your kingdom as if we were readers
in some great library,
with always something new to discover there.

O Jesus, King most wonderful:
teach us to recognise our fellow citizens and our King

in the folk of the Bible and the folk of every day
– instant neighbours,
like passport-holders from the same country meeting
     abroad.

O Jesus, King most wonderful:
teach us the faith
in which your kingdom's miracles are wrought;
may the victories of love and truth we hope for
begin to take shape and substance in what we do.

We ask these things
in your royal name.

d. 'Forth in thy name'

19

The Album

'Leave your troubles with the Lord . . .'   Ps 55:22

God our Father: with amazing grace you have invited us
into an intimacy where we can open our minds to you
as we might show an album of pictures to a friend.

Look, this is our home and the family, those are
     neighbours,
here are colleagues with whom it is a pleasure to work
– and some with whom it is not.

Here are tasks to finish, and some not yet begun:

humdrum, repetitive, unavoidable chores, daily,
    unremitting,
so that we can get a living and keep a home together.

Look what worries us – our real responsibilities:
school clothes, housekeeping, rent, mortgage, debts
    and taxes,
family health, and keeping the peace when tempers
    fray.

Then here are some things we worry about
because someone has taught us to worry about them:
the economy, the third world, and war in south-east
    somewhere

– the world's a village, everyone's our neighbour,
but we're still not sure quite how to respond to distant
    news,
propaganda ours and theirs, relief fund appeals,
    Amnesty. . . .

Lord God: here we are in a world which looks like this,
living a life which looks like this.
We need you with us; others need you too.

Enter the world you made and we inhabit: come in, do.
Abide with us, for our day and we are far spent
trying to go it alone.

Forgive the sins of the world, and especially our share;
give strength to do the things we should and can do,
and eyes to see what they are.

Give us courage to act for good wherever possible,
whether our action seems important or not;

give us patience with the things and people
we cannot hope to change;

help all who are trying to do your will
to do it better.

And into all the dark places of the world
where we cannot go

carrying the light,
there let our prayers go,
and your grace,
your power,
your love.

Make our world your world again, Lord God;
and give peace in our time,

through Jesus Christ.

20

The Divine Pity

'As kind as a father is to his children . . .'   Ps 103:13

O God, you are the Father of Jesus
in whom we see a patient and effective compassion
– a picture of your own compassion:
  he pardoned atrocious sinners,
  he lit up hopeless minds,
  he cured terrible diseases,
  he taught people who were exasperatingly slow to
    learn.
Miracles like these and more
he performed in response
to pathetically little faith
on the part of pathetically few believers.
  O God, we are not many, and our faith is not great,
  but in Jesus' name we turn to you
  for just such miracles.

All around us human folly throws away
things we say we value:
  men who fear unemployment and poverty go on
    strike,
  making more certain the poverty and unemployment
  which they fear.
  A peace conference meets,

and its members at once fall to fighting again
because they cannot agree the agenda.
Terrorists complain that a people is oppressed,
and make their point by oppressing the same people
with bondage to constant fear,
in the name of liberation.

O God, we ask
for a new outpouring of commonsense, clear sight and
    patience.
Help us to secure peace
by multiplying kindness instead of arms
– kindness for people we can help tomorrow,
    instead of overkill for people we might dislike next
        week.
Set nations busy feeding hungry children,
                    educating the ignorant,
                    healing the sick.
Cure the prosperous of their greed,
and the disadvantaged of their spite.

Make a miracle in the minds of rulers,
so that policies may be for *people*
    rather than for profit or prestige:
what needs doing
    rather than what will look good.
Comfort the hearts of ordinary folk,
and make it possible for them to trust their leaders.
Sweeten with kindness and courage
the day-to-day business of life.

We who count ourselves your people, by your grace,
ask you to bless and guide our friendships,
our loves and our homes.

Help us by your grace
to live as those who have been given the right
to be called children of God,
through Jesus Christ.

21

Really for Us

'. . . all who ask the Lord for help will be saved.'   Joel 2:32

Lord God:
convince us that your love in Christ is FOR US.
Thrill us with the knowledge that YOU CARE for us,
that your desire is TO SAVE us – EACH ONE,
none too insignificant, none too bad
for your mercy to restore.

★

Then set our faces aglow and our tongues wagging
with the GOOD NEWS.

22

In his Hands

'O Lord, you have always been our home.'   Ps 90:1

Great God:
you are eternal, you know the end from the beginning;
our times are in your hands, and that is where we want
    them.
Give us each day our share of the bread
and our share of the action.
Take into your great purpose our little lives,
forgive our sins and light our path;
so that,
in the peace which you give
and the world cannot take away,
we may trust where we cannot see,
and lovingly obey where we cannot understand;
by the grace of Jesus Christ our Lord.

23

Escaping from Ourselves

'. . . look out for one another's interests, not just for your own.'
Phil 2:4

In all the busyness of our daily life,
Lord God,
keep us mindful of yourself
and of our fellow men and women.

★

Keep our vision clear
and our ears quick
for things and people
beyond our own immediate preoccupations, passions,
prides and despairs.

★

So,
humbly and usefully abiding in your love,
and accepting such prosperity as you allow,
may we know a peace
which the world can neither give nor take away,
according to the promise
of Jesus your Son,
in whose name we pray.

24

Commission

'As the Father sent me, so I send you.'   Jn 20:21

Lord God:
one of our hymns calls the Church 'unequal to her task',
and we know that, apart from your grace,
she is completely unable to do what you ask of her.
We also know that what matters

is not her inadequacy but your commission.
What you command you also make possible,
for you do not tease your children.
You have given to your apostles and to those who
    follow them
authority to preach and heal and cast out demons.

★

Give to your Church here and now
the word you want spoken
to our town (**), its leaders and its people.
By the gift of your Holy Spirit,
make each church member able to live and speak
as ambassador to (*) from the high court of heaven.
Give us the word of judgment and reconciliation.
Do through our hands your deeds of healing and love.
Your will be done on earth as it is in heaven,
beginning with us, in the place where we live,
in the community we can affect;
for your glory we ask it,
and in the name of Jesus Christ, our Saviour,
and the Saviour of all.

25
Advance

'. . . whoever believes in me . . . will do even greater things . . .'
Jn 14:12

O God, we praise you for being alive in your Church.
We know it is not our buildings or organisations
which show that you are alive,
but our outgoing love, our ongoing mission,
our continuing growth.
Keep us for ever discontented

**City etc   *Place Name

with the progress we have so far let you make in us.
Make us more open to your Spirit
and more obedient to your will.
Be with your missionary Church throughout the world,
and make us your missionary Church here.
Keep in our minds the vision of ourselves
as your advancing army,
with the gates of hell already crumbling
as our marching feet shake the ground.
Keep us always attempting greater things for you
and expecting greater things from you.
Fill us with the fervent and venturing Spirit
of him in whose name we pray,
Jesus Christ our Lord.

26

Rest

'Come to me, all of you who are tired . . .'   Mt 11:28

Heavenly Father:
we thank you for rest,
and for the honest weariness
which makes us ready to enjoy resting.
We thank you for leisure
and for the energy and the interests
which enable us to fill leisure with refreshment and
          profit.
Especially we thank you
for that relaxation from fear and from selfish striving
promised to those who place the direction of their lives
in your hands.

★

Enable us, O God, to glorify you
in our work and in our leisure.
And give us grace to offer for your use
even the enforced rest of illness and age,

redundancy and unemployment.
So in all our life
may your Spirit be preparing us
for an eternity of joy in your presence,
where our promised rest
shall be tireless service
and unceasing praise;
through Jesus Christ our Lord.

27

Realism

'Trust in the Lord. Have faith. Do not despair.'   Ps 27:14

Give to your servants, O God,
a quiet confidence
in your ability
to bring about
the good things you have promised.
Give us courage to attempt great things in your service;
give us faith to expect great things from your grace.
Give us patience to wait for your time.

★

Make us humble before the realities of earthly life
– for we would not be deluded
   into thinking that the human condition
   is better than it is –
but keep us obstinate in believing
that everything good is possible
through Jesus Christ our Lord.

28
Abundance

'You fill my cup to the brim.'   Ps 23:5

Heavenly Father:
you give us things to delight in,
you give us people to care for,
you give us a Saviour and King to follow and serve,
you give us through him tasks to do and time to use,
you give us, as he promised, the Holy Spirit to help us.
Give us also,
now and always,
your blessing for his sake.

29
Responsibility

'There was once a man who planted a vineyard, let it out to
tenants . . .'   Lk 20:9

O GOD,
    giver of the world we live in,
    giver of the air we breathe,
    giver of seedtime and harvest,
    giver of life:
FORGIVE US for living as though we were not
    dependent on you
    and as though we were the only ones who
    mattered.
TEACH US to care about your world and your *other*
    people;
    remind us that we live as tenants on your estate;
    cure our greed;
    may we find pleasure in simple things,
    and joy in sharing.
WE PRAY for all who have not yet a fair share
    of your world's goods;

help us to help them however we can.
ABOVE ALL help us and all mankind
to discover the new world and the fullness of life
which you open up to us
in Jesus Christ our Lord.

30

Conviction

'. . . nothing you do in the Lord's service is ever useless.'   1 Cor 15:58

God, give us the faith to believe
what we say we believe,
and the courage to live by it.
Convince us and keep us convinced
that you exist and love us;
that you know the worst about us
and love us just the same;
that you have forgiven our sins;
that you know the tragic power of death
and have defeated it;
that for those who trust you,
eternal life has now begun;
that in the end
all your loving purpose for the universe
will be fulfilled;
and that meanwhile
no effort toward truth and goodness is
wasted,
since human love and what it achieves
endures,
and is precious in your sight.
Lord, we believe;
increase our faith
through the grace of Jesus Christ.

31

Dismissal

'And I will be with you always . . .'   Mt 28:20

Thank you, Father, for all the words
which we have said and sung and listened to:
the story and celebration of your power –
> the faith of the psalmists,
> the hope of the prophets,
> the joy of the first Christians, witnesses
> > of Christ's resurrection
> > > to whom he was made known, risen and
> > > > alive,
> > in the breaking of bread.
Thank you for the music, the prayer and the
> preaching –
> > > all telling us again that you are great,
> > > that you are on our side,
> > > that everything is in your hands
> > > and that all will be well.
We confess there is a problem here, almighty God:
we don't always feel as confident
> or sound so impressive
> or look so strong,
> once we are out of church again
> facing the everyday world.
We have doubts there, heavenly Father,
and we make compromises,
we fear for the future,
even the future of your Church
– we, who sing your greatness on Sundays!

Help us, dear Father God,
to know the reality of YOU amidst the realities of daily
> life
> > – business, work, home, school,
> > social change and political uncertainty.
Help us to know there, and then, and always,

your power, your victory and your presence with us.

We don't just want to be religious people
who think good thoughts on Sunday,
but saints of God and citizens of heaven,
bearing Christ's cross and sharing Christ's victory
every day of the week;
we want to be involved with you
in the redemption of the world.
Almighty Father, show us how
and make it happen
through Christ's grace,
for we ask it in his name.

INDEX OF PRAYERS

Listed each with keynote text, the scripture passage giving its context, and sequence of secondary references.

BEGINNING

a. to church with a purpose

b. thanks, praise & joy

c. the need for pardon

d. what we believe

'FAMILY CHURCH'

a. all together

b. thank you, God

c. living thanks

d. the Lord Jesus

e. think, then pray

OFFERING

a. at Communion

b. with thanks

INTERCESSION

a. about the Church

b. about people

c. about problems

COMMITMENT & PETITION

a. as worship begins

b. after readings

c. after hymns

d.   'Forth in thy name'

INDEX OF KEYNOTE TEXTS
and context passages

Note Each verse and context passage given here is the one which as the prayer it is attached to evolved seemed to set its key. But for a particular purpose – for instance in choosing a reading to precede or follow a prayer, one of the secondary references in small type in the Index of Prayers may be found more useful.

6:35   (6:26–58)   *Offering* **3**
6:68   (6:60–69)   *Family Church* **8**
10:9   (10:1–9)   *Family Church* **12**
14:1   (14 & 15)   *Commitment & Petition* **8**
14:6   (14:4–7)   *Family Church* **2**
14:12   (14:11–17)   *Commitment & Petition* **25**
15:5   (15:1–17)   *Offering* **21**
15:26   (15:26–16:5)   *Intercession* **14**
19:11   (19:1–16)   *Intercession* **21**
20:21   (20:19–23)   *Commitment & Petition* **24**
20:31   (20:24–31)   *Family Church* **22**
21:17   (21:15–25)   *Commitment & Petition* **9**

Romans
8:28   (8:18–30)   *Offering* **8**
12:1   (12:1–13)   *Offering* **13**
12:2   (12:1–2)   *Commitment & Petition* **10**
12:11, 13   (12:1–13)   *Offering* **12**
14:5   (14:1–19)   *Family Church* **11**
15:13   (15:1–13)   *Beginning* **18**

1 Corinthians
3:10   (3:9–17)   *Beginning* **22**
5:7   (5:6–8)   *Offering* **16**
11:17   (11:17–34)   *Intercession* **9**
15:58   (15:12–58)   *Commitment & Petition* **30**
16:2–3 (16:1–4)   *Offering* **11**

2 Corinthians
5:17   (5:11–12)   *Commitment & Petition* **16**
11:28   (11:16–29)   *Intercession* **7**
12:9   (12:1–10)   *Family Church* **14**

Ephesians
3:14–15   (3:14–21)   *Beginning* **5**
3:17   (3:14–21)   *Commitment & Petition* **11**
3:21   (3:14–21)   *Beginning* **3**
4:12   (4:7–12 or 4:1–16)   *Offering* **22**
4:16   (4:1–16)   *Offering* **23**
4:26   (4:21b–27)   *Family Church* **24**

Philippians
1:5   (1:3–11)   *Offering* **6**

A SUBJECT INDEX

INDEX OF RELATED HYMNS